T0357971

HACK IN A
FLAK JACKET

HACK IN A FLAK JACKET

WARS, RIOTS AND REVOLUTIONS
DISPATCHES FROM A FOREIGN CORRESPONDENT

PETER STEFANOVIC

hachette
AUSTRALIA

First published in Australia and New Zealand in 2016
by Hachette Australia
(an imprint of Hachette Australia Pty Limited)
Level 17, 207 Kent Street, Sydney NSW 2000
www.hachette.com.au

This edition published in 2017

10 9 8 7 6 5 4 3 2 1

National Library of Australia
Cataloguing-in-Publication data

Stefanovic, Peter, author.
Hack in a flak jacket / Peter Stefanovic.

978 0 7336 3878 7 (paperback)

Stefanovic, Peter.
Foreign correspondents – Australia – Biography.
Television journalists – Australia – Biography.

070.92

Cover design by Luke Causby
Front cover photograph courtesy of Shaun Filer; back cover photograph courtesy of James Gillings
Text design by Bookhouse, Sydney
Typeset in 11.75/18.5 pt Sabon Pro by Bookhouse, Sydney
Printed and bound in Australia by McPherson's Printing Group

To Jenny Penny

CONTENTS

PROLOGUE

Flak jackets are dreadful things. Sure, they have a purpose, and if one ever stopped a bullet or piece of shrapnel from spearing into my vital organs, I would kiss it, hang it up, and frame it. But that hasn't happened, yet. So far, most of my dealings with them have been negative. Wearing them in the dry deserts of the Middle East and North Africa, where the climate is a positively balmy 800 degrees. Putting up with the tight canvas and large plates of heavy metal tucked into the front and back that make you walk like a sweaty Robocop but not look nearly as cool.

Yep, the old trusty flak jacket is a sight to behold, and has also been responsible for what may be the most embarrassing moment of my time as a foreign correspondent.

It was in the Libyan capital of Tripoli in the middle of 2011. The country's brutal dictator, Colonel Muammar Gaddafi, who had been in power for more than forty years, had finally been chased out of town by an opposition hungry for his blood. The city was still in the midst of a civil war between government and rebel forces.

I was standing in the driveway of the Corinthia Hotel, where we were staying, when all of a sudden these big angry guards armed to the teeth started firing their automatic weapons at the building across the road. TUT-TUT-TUT-TUT-TUT-TUT. The jarring sound of gunfire rocketed across the street.

There are moments in life when you think, 'I really could have done that better.' This was one of those instances. While my cameraman James Gillings filmed the moment flawlessly, I tried to get back into the hotel as quickly as possible. So did the other twenty or so jumpy journalists nearby, all of us trying to squeeze through a single door at the hotel entrance at the same time.

The gunfire continued. The rebels at our hotel were shouting at government snipers who were supposedly firing at them from the other side of the street.

I finally burst through the front door, but then tripped spectacularly and faceplanted the hard marble floor of the foyer. A completely graceless, self-inflicted body slam.

I thought the snipers were about to invade the hotel so I desperately tried to get back on my feet. But because the soles of my boots were worn and the armour in my flak jacket was sliding across the slippery floor, I just couldn't get up. All I could see were the feet of other journalists scurrying past me and running for cover, while I was in the middle of the hotel lobby reminding everyone what a turtle looked like when it's stuck on its back. Although technically I was on my stomach, so go figure.

After a few more mad moments of panic, I finally got to my feet and bolted to the nearest available hiding spot – a large pot plant near the concierge desk. Beads of sweat were pouring down my face and I caught the eye of a British journalist close by. 'That was pretty funny, mate,' he said.

Cheers.

My name is Peter Stefanovic. Just a hack in a flak jacket.

Chapter 1

THERE WILL BE BLOOD

GAZA AND ISRAEL

There were three deep thuds in the distance. BOOM. BOOM. BOOM. They came from the Mediterranean Sea and sounded like a heavy bass drum. Barely half a second later, deathly missiles screamed past my window and set off an almighty explosion – once, twice, thrice. The target next door to my hotel vaporised. Blown to bits.

It was a dark and balmy night, but through the glass door of my room I could see a huge fiery mushroom cloud lighting up the sky. Israeli warships had taken out what they believed were Hamas targets less than a hundred metres from where I had been sleeping. Whatever the shells had struck, there was nothing left of it now, and if anyone had been there ... well, they wouldn't be anymore.

The sheer power of the explosions was so strong that the entire hotel I was in shook as if in an earthquake, and

1

a hail of sharp metal shrapnel speared into my windows. A few pieces managed to barrel through a slight opening of the balcony's sliding door. I picked one up off the floor. It was still searing and it burned my hand. Sharp, heavy and hot. When moving very fast, shrapnel is like jagged bullets. Lethal.

A minute passed, and an eerie silence returned to the night. Then three more loud thuds from the Med – same sound, same spot. I knew what was coming, so I dived to the floor and into a tiny space that separated the two single beds in the middle of my room. It would have looked comical if it weren't so serious. Death was on its way again.

A sliver of time passed before a loud cacophony of quick, high-pitched whistles went by as three more rockets flew past, rattling my windows before impact. BOOM. BOOM. BOOM. The earth shook, my building swayed, another close target up in smoke.

The explosions rumbled on for hours. Different targets, different noises, different weapons. Incoming fire, outgoing fire.

Welcome to Gaza.

•

It was November 2012. The day before the explosions shook my hotel, I had been in Israel, heading to the Gaza Strip for the first time to report on the escalating tension between Israelis and Palestinians. I had been working as Channel Nine's foreign correspondent for Europe, the Middle East and Africa since 2010 and, although I was based in London,

I spent a lot of time travelling around the region. That's half the world I covered together with my cameraman, and in a news sense it was a fertile patch. When a major story flashed across the news wires or came into the newsroom in London, I phoned editors in Sydney who would green-light the assignment. Air tickets, hotel rooms, and translators were booked and we were off. At a conservative estimate I was away from home at least 50 per cent of the time.

I had been to Israel before, in January 2009 during a similar nasty conflict known (by the Israelis) as Operation Cast Lead and (by the Palestinians) as the Gaza massacre, but back then Israel's government prevented most Western journalists from entering the Gaza Strip. Perhaps they were concerned for our lives. Perhaps they didn't want us to see what was going on. We covered that conflict from the border.

Israel, Gaza, and the West Bank lie on what is perhaps the most hotly contested piece of land on the planet. Arabic and Jewish people lay claim to the Holy Land and have fought over it for thousands of years. It's a complicated, brutal history mostly based on religion and divine right that is much better explained by historians than me. In 2012, tensions were centred on the control Israel had over Gaza and the territorial restrictions it had imposed on the area that meant supplies and aid were prevented from entering or leaving the Strip by land, sea, or air. It is a very tricky conflict for journalists to cover because different people feel so passionately about it and we are often criticised for being too one-sided – pro-Israel or pro-Palestine. I have spent time with people on both sides of the conflict and I feel for them all.

In the days before I arrived in the region, Palestinian militants in Gaza had sharply increased the amount of rockets and mortar shells they were launching into Israel, and Israel had stepped up its response. An Israeli airstrike had killed a Hamas leader in Gaza. Israel had a massive military machine at its disposal. Its army, weaponry, and technology were more powerful and far more advanced than Gaza's. It wasn't even a contest. So when Israel decided to respond, it didn't muck around.

I was given fair warning that going to Gaza would be a dangerous assignment – to cover the story properly meant my life would probably be threatened. But I felt that people needed to know what was happening across the iron fence that separated Gaza from Israel. We needed to see the scale of devastation and the human cost that accompanied it.

So on 17 November 2012, two days before my thirty-first birthday, I made it to the Erez crossing, Israel's high security border with Gaza. The crossing consisted of a huge dull building on barren land, which was connected to the high barbed-wire fence that surrounded the Strip. This was what stood between northern Gaza and southern Israel, which was restricted to Arab residents and closed to tourists. Palestinians who had permits to work in Israel, or who were allowed to receive medical treatment or visit family members who were in prisons, could sometimes use the crossing when it was open for pedestrian travel. It could take a pounding during times of war and, when the heat was on, it could close for days or even weeks. No one got in. No one got out.

A middle-aged Jewish lady appeared to be very pensive as she closely examined passports, and crosschecked them with the hopeful faces of journalists who stared back at her. I'm sure she thought we were crazy, or stupid, or both. People were nervous around Gaza. But then again, people were nervous across the entire region.

I walked up to her booth. She looked at me, then looked down at my passport and media card, and looked up at me again the same way my neighbour looks at me whenever I put my rubbish in his bin. 'I see it is your birthday in two days,' she said in a thick Hebrew accent.

'That's right,' I said.

Her expression lightened slightly. 'Well, at least you will get your own fireworks!' She laughed at her quip. I laughed too, but more out of nervousness. She allowed me through, and my heartbeat started to quicken.

For this assignment, I had been teamed up with cameraman James Gillings. The only clothes we had were the ones on our backs. We weren't sure how long we would be in Gaza so we only wanted to carry a light load – in case we needed to move fast. Camera, tripod, a few cases of lighting and broadcasting equipment, a computer to file our stories and, of course, armour – helmets and flak jackets. We were advised to put them on immediately, and duly obliged. But just before we drifted into no-man's-land we were given some last-minute pointers.

'Please try and make sure you are visible to us,' we were told by the Israeli security officials. 'Put a press badge on your flak jacket, and when travelling mark the roof or bonnet of your car with a large "TV" in black tape so the drones can see.' This, we were told, might prevent a large bomb from landing near us or, even worse, on us. The security bloke was actually quite charming and appeared to be genuinely concerned for us. He wished us well and hoped to see us soon, alive if possible. Gallows humour at its finest.

Gaza began the moment we passed through huge iron doors that led to an old, somewhat-rusted, full-body turn-stile, which we had to feed our equipment through piece by piece, and then lastly squeeze ourselves through. Next we arrived at a long, caged concrete walkway that stretched for about 400 metres across brown and sandy barren country and took us to the top of the Gaza Strip. The soundtrack to our journey consisted of drones buzzing overhead, and rockets landing here and there. It was a very unsettling walk.

Crossing from Israel into Gaza is a remarkable transition, like entering a completely different world. Israel is largely clean, and has a healthy mixture of modern and ancient architecture. Gaza is dry, dusty and dirty, and sewage gives it a rotten smell in parts. Although some areas are beautiful, especially along coastal beaches that could be surfed with a long board, with 1.8 million people stacked into the

Strip, it's mostly built up and cramped. People call it the world's largest open-air prison. You cannot be guaranteed absolute safety.

My friend and Australian *60 Minutes* cameraman, Andy Taylor, had suggested I call a lady named Ameera Harouda when I arrived in Gaza. He hadn't met her but had heard she was someone local who potentially could help us get around and operate in Gaza. Foreign correspondents call people like this 'fixers'. Without them, we are useless. There is a saying that on the ground you are only as good as your fixer and, believe me, it's true. I've had good ones and bad ones. Ameera was a good one, and I trusted her from the start.

She arranged for James and me to be picked up as soon as we emerged from the caged walkway. Drenched in sweat, and already worn out, we had our passport details taken by a group of men I assumed to be members of Hamas. At the time, Hamas was both a governing body of the Gaza Strip and a military organisation led by the al-Qassam Brigades. Hamas is an Arabic acronym, which in English means 'the Islamic Resistance Movement'. It was formed in 1987 at the beginning of the First Intifada, which was a Palestinian uprising against perceived Israeli oppression. But because of suicide bombings and terror attacks it's become known by many countries as a terrorist group.

We were driven to our hotel in a small yellow run-down sedan. Ameera had told our driver to take the back route to avoid buildings that would likely be targeted by Israeli bombs and rockets. I could see the joint was already a mess. As we travelled along dirt roads, we passed large bomb craters in the ground and homes that had tumbled to their foundations.

It was getting late in the day and I needed to file something for the next major news bulletin in Australia. We had to file several reports every day. One for the morning news, one for the lunchtime edition, and one for the evening bulletin. So, after we checked into the hotel, one of Ameera's friends took us on a little drive through the streets. We stopped near a collapsed government building so I could film a piece to camera. I figured that since the building had already been hit, it wouldn't need to be hit again so we would be safe.

Moments after James finished recording my piece to camera, we heard a fast-moving, loud rumble coming our way. In a split second the roar of a military jet passed over our heads, and a bomb dropped on a building a few hundred metres away. The noise was deafening, and it happened so fast. In the time it took us just to look to the sky in response to the noise, a huge column of dark smoke was already rising from the bomb's destination and the jet had vanished in the distance. Lives were gone in an instant.

My heart was thumping wildly. The microphone locked on my chest was probably picking up the heavy beats. We'd been in Gaza for just a few hours, and already we'd felt the full impact and jarring fury of war.

James and I weren't adrenaline junkies, but by that stage we had covered several of the so-called Arab Spring uprisings in 2011 when Tunisians, Egyptians and Libyans booted out their governments, so we had a bit of experience. We jumped in the car, and sped directly to the smoke and the fire.

It was chaos. A ten-storey building had been obliterated. We arrived to find men screaming, and women howling. Scattered helpers ran every which way, unsure of what exactly to do. Paramedics were pulling bodies out of the rubble. I saw the lifeless limbs of a child wrapped in a blanket as it was rushed to a waiting ambulance, along with dead and wounded that were carried on pieces of carpet.

There was a huge pile of debris where the bomb had struck. Broken bits of brick and concrete were tangled with cables and wire. I climbed to the top and peered into a massive smouldering crater where the building had once stood, where people had once lived and laughed. Ten storeys high was now ten storeys low. James met me at the top of this mountain of ruin and filmed the desperate search for survivors. But people took offence at the filming and began to pelt him with rocks. We got the message and quickly shuffled away.

Despite the obvious despair at the bomb site, there was also a massive undercurrent of seething outrage. The people shouted 'Allahu Akbar' (God is great). Ten people had been killed. Their lives lost in a flash. Israel later claimed the building was a base for Hamas operatives who were co-ordinating and planning attacks across the border. But they were wrong. It was later proven that it was a family of innocent civilians who were lost in the fog of war. Israel took a rare step and apologised.

James and I had experienced conflict, but never at such close quarters. It was a lot to absorb. So much death and destruction on one sunny afternoon. But there was much worse to come.

We went back to our hotel and filed what we thought was a powerful story. We were tired, but sleep didn't come. Because then it started. That deep drum from the ocean. *BOOM. BOOM. BOOM.*

•

I was awoken by an explosion so frightening and so powerful that it felt like my heart had leapt out of my chest. I took a huge and hurried gulp of air as I tried to collect my thoughts and remember where I was. Gaza. My building was shaking yet again but the sound was much louder this time and it came with a force much stronger than any of the other explosions I'd heard. It was just after six in the morning.

About a kilometre away from our hotel, a Palestinian government building where some police work was carried out was smashed by an airstrike. It was a large building so it required a few bombs to destroy the whole thing. Hence the bigger bang that was heard across the Strip. The occupants had been warned that the missiles were coming, so the building was empty at the time of the blast. Debris – including dozens of burnt flags, office stationery and furniture, and personal effects – was scattered over a vast area.

It may sound insensitive, but after a few days in Gaza the damage all started to look the same. Ameera suggested I spend a day with some paramedics she knew. These were the people who bravely rushed to the sites of bomb blasts, putting their own lives at risk to try to save the wounded. Ambulances were often targeted in strikes so accompanying the paramedics was a huge risk, but James and I thought it was an important story to tell.

Paramedics astound me. They are brave and tremendously selfless people. My great-grandfather on my mother's side – Private George Alwyn Little (who many years later would help the Reverend Alan Walker establish Lifeline in Sydney) – was a stretcher-bearer on the Western Front in World War I. His father, my great-great-grandfather, George Little, was a courageous lighterman on England's River Lea who had rescued fifty-six people by the time he died of natural causes – ironically, while on a stretcher – at sixty-three years of age. So the humble paramedic, the lifesaver as it were, is a job I have always admired and been fascinated by.

On the day we accompanied the paramedics in Gaza, there happened to be a lull in the fighting. I was lying on the dirt road, waiting, using my helmet as a pillow, my eyes trailing the many drones that were circling us in the sky above. They weren't hard to find. Little white moving objects that sounded like angry hornets buzzing high up. I watched them as they watched me. A few boys on an apple cart whipped a haggard donkey down the road. Young opportunists out to make a buck while school was off. I waved to them, and they smiled back. Hours passed.

It was quiet. Eerily so. A few of the paramedics sat in the shade and sipped cups of sweet tea. They chatted away in Arabic, a language I wished I could speak, and I slowly started to drift off to sleep.

The silence was broken by a loud bang and then the phone calls came in. There was a drone strike to the east of the city, and our crew was closest and urgently needed. The paramedics gesticulated for James and me to get in the back of the ambulance. No Arabic needed. No one gesticulates better than the Arabs, not even the Italians. We were soon on our way.

A million thoughts rushed through my mind as the ambulance sped down the road. This was dangerous. Could there be a second strike? Did the attack come from the drone I had been watching? Could we be hit? What would we see? How many would be dead?

In the front, the drivers madly barked at one another. Were they scared too? I often thought that if a shell ever struck me I probably wouldn't feel it. I hoped I wouldn't anyway.

There were no speed limits in Gaza but plenty of speed bumps, and the ambulance crashed into them at high speeds, which sent medical supplies flying, and James and me sliding off our seats.

A few frantic minutes passed before we arrived at the scene. The sliding door of the ambulance was thrown open and we got out to find a farmhouse had been hit. Why? We never found out. But wounded victims were lying on the burnt grass and people were frantically rushing about trying to help. We followed the paramedics as they ran through the shocked and confused crowd until they stopped and picked up a young man who had severe head injuries. They lifted him up, carried him to the ambulance, and placed his flimsy body on a gurney. Men were shouting at each other but all I could do was stare at the man's face. He looked so young, in his late teens or early twenties, with a whole life ahead of him. I thought he was dead but was told he wasn't, not yet anyway.

We climbed into the back of the ambulance and shut the door as the motor revved and the vehicle tore off down the road on its way back to the main al-Shifa hospital. James filmed as a paramedic desperately tried to save the young man. I watched as the medic tried to stop the bleeding. There wasn't much room, so the blood was gushing off the young man's head and onto my boots and legs. The medic was getting frustrated as he cut the man's shirt open and wiped beads of sweat from his own brow. He was determined to keep the young man alive, even as the ambulance's high speed caused the body to shift around on the gurney.

A few minutes later we stopped and the back doors were thrust open. A blinding light filled the ambulance as doctors grabbed the young man and rushed him into the hospital's emergency room. Dozens of news cameras flashed and rolled.

Most of the journalists and cameramen who visited Gaza stayed at the hospital because rockets didn't land there. Israeli officials believed Hamas militants based themselves inside the hospital because they knew it wouldn't be attacked. I thought the Israelis were probably right, but I could never confirm it. I often saw people at the hospital cheer, though, when a departing rocket was launched from an area close by and sailed towards Israel, leaving a white trail of smoke in its wake. 'God is great,' the people would shout.

James and I got out of the ambulance and were left with a bloodstained gurney as the paramedics sped off to pick up more victims. Off they went again, the heroes of the day. But we had seen enough. Still to this day, I don't know if that young man survived.

•

After a few days in Gaza we could tell the difference between the sounds of Grad missiles, Qassam rockets, mortar shells, and airstrikes. Those that were coming in, and those that were heading out. We even got used to the buzz of the drones. As Ameera told me, it was when the drones couldn't be heard that people grew nervous.

I ended up having my birthday in Gaza on 19 November. James had smuggled in a bottle of Jameson whiskey in our tripod case. Alcohol was forbidden in Gaza, as it was in many Arabic countries. I remember sitting with James on the balcony, sipping away as we looked at the city's night lights, when all of a sudden the warship fired again.

BOOM. BOOM. BOOM. A triple pack of missiles roared right past us. James and I crashed into each other as we both scrambled to get inside the room. I smashed my toes on the door railing as I dived inside just as the shrapnel pinged against the balcony railing.

A few moments later, once the threat had passed, we looked at each other and laughed. Our hands might have been shaking, but we didn't spill a single drop. At times like those, whiskey was liquid gold.

A footnote on the topic of liquid refreshment is that I drank a lot of Coca-Cola in the Middle East, and formed a theory on its effectiveness as a germ killer. We ate a lot of street food on the run, and as delicious as it was, I often couldn't be sure it was clean. So I always washed down my meals with a can of Coke, and I never became ill.

•

On 21 November, just two days after my birthday, Israeli and Palestinian authorities agreed to a ceasefire, which was brokered by the United States and Egypt. After almost a week in Gaza, seeing the daily destruction and listening to missiles roaring past my balcony, I was not only tired but emotionally drained. I couldn't imagine what it must be like for the people who lived in Gaza permanently.

Before we left for Tel Aviv in Israel, James and I had dinner with Ameera and her family. Their home was small but neat and comfortable. She had bought us some fish that had been caught in the small section of sea that Israel allowed Palestinian fishermen to operate in. If they started to cross the boundary, warning shots were usually fired at them. It was part of the tension that had built up in the region over the years.

It was the best meal I'd had in days, and Ameera was relaxed because the bombs had stopped. I asked her what she told her two young children when the war was raging outside. Her answer has stayed with me. She said she tells them there's a party outside, and the bombs and rockets are just fireworks, so there's nothing to be afraid of.

We said our goodbyes, and wished each other well. It wouldn't be long, though, before I saw them again.

•

Barely eighteen months passed before Israel and Palestine were at it again. Despite the ceasefire, differences had not been resolved and restrictions hadn't eased, so the rockets flew once more. The tipping point came on 12 June 2014, when three Israeli teenagers were kidnapped and killed by Hamas militants in the West Bank. It triggered a chain of events that ultimately led to the deaths of more than 2200 Palestinians and over eighty Israelis, most of whom were soldiers.

One minute I was on holidays sailing on a boat with friends in Italy, the next I was on a plane heading back into the Middle East to report on events. Same story, different cameraman – this time Luke Wilson was capturing the images.

Since 2011, Israel had an extraordinary piece of military hardware called the Iron Dome missile defence system. If Hamas launched a rocket over the Israeli border, it was detected by radar, which triggered a loud siren to alert people to get into bomb shelters, and within a few seconds an intercepting rocket was launched from Israel's side to crash mid-air into the incoming rocket. It was extremely high tech, expensive, and very impressive. It had saved many lives over the years but was not always successful.

While they were still deadly and had plenty of range, Palestinian rockets had nowhere near the capabilities of Israeli rockets. They were often provided by countries such as Iran or Syria – more enemies of Israel – and usually smuggled into Gaza through a vast network of underground tunnels. Since Israel imposed restrictions on what could be imported into Gaza, much of what reached the Strip came through the concrete tunnels – weapons, cars, livestock, food, water, medicine, and building supplies.

Hamas militants had also been using the tunnels to launch surprise raids on Israeli military bases, not all that far from the kibbutz we stayed in, in towns including Ashkelon and Ashdod. A kibbutz is an Israeli settlement where groups of families live. When we were in Israel, we usually stayed in those towns because they were closer to Gaza. Rockets would often target them. When the siren was triggered by an incoming missile, we'd have to scurry off into small bomb shelters and wait. When the rocket landed and its warhead exploded close by we'd hear a loud boom, and if they were really close, the ground would shake. Sometimes the rockets would make it as far north as the highly populated city of Tel Aviv.

One such rocket snuck through the Iron Dome defence system and speared into a high-rise apartment building just south of Tel Aviv. We travelled to the site to see what had happened, and to get some footage for the evening news bulletin in Australia. The damage to the apartment block was significant, although fortunately no one was home at the time of the blast. As I inspected the damage, I spoke to a woman named Dina Lasri who lived next door, and asked her what life was like under the threat of Hamas rockets. Right at that precise moment, a loud siren blared to tell us a Palestinian rocket was on its way. We scrambled into the closest bomb shelter and closed the door. Ms Lasri started softly weeping into her hands. The tension was palpable but I asked her about it anyway. 'Always we live like this,' she said. 'Always. I worry about my family. It's my home. It's very frightening.' There was a thud in the distance, the missile was intercepted, and 'life' resumed.

In the few days we stayed in Israel's south, I saw the same story over and over again – homes or kibbutz smashed by rockets, cars struck on streets, windows shattered by missile shrapnel, and people killed, although the death toll was always considerably lower in Israel because of the Iron Dome.

As tensions increased and a higher number of rockets sailed both ways, it was time for us to re-enter the Gaza

Strip so we could capture both sides of the story for the viewers in Australia. We knew it was going to be dangerous, but we didn't know that a fifty-day war was about to erupt and Palestinians would suffer the most casualties since the Six-Day War in 1967.

•

The day I returned to Gaza was the day a story broke that shocked the world. It was 16 July 2014, a few days into the Israeli offensive known as Operation Protective Edge. Four kids from the same family had been playing on the Gaza City Harbour Beach when Israeli shells, launched from a nearby gunboat, killed them. A fishing shack near a pier had been blown up first, and photographs showed the boys running for cover. But then Ahed Bakr, Zakaria Bakr, and two other boys both named Mohammad Bakr were shot dead. The oldest was just eleven years of age. Israel thought the children were militants but was proven wrong once pictures and eyewitness accounts emerged from several foreign journalists who'd been staying at a hotel close by.

I was at the hospital when the boys' mothers arrived to identify the bodies. Never have I seen emotion so raw and so heartbreaking. I watched the women howl – a primal scream that still resonates with me today. One of the mothers dropped to her knees and angrily shouted at the sky, while others passed out and collapsed on the ground.

I found a Hamas representative close by and asked her what the deaths would mean for relations with Israel. She told me in no uncertain terms, 'There is no peace with Israel. Israel must pay for this.'

The hospital was quickly becoming a place for prayers and tears. On any day during the war its wards were full of wounded bodies and souls. Bandaged limbs and faces. I sat with one man who had been struck by the debris caused by a bomb. His face was so battered that his friend had to slowly squeeze water into his mouth through a syringe.

In the next room I spoke with a father named Ibrahim el Masri, who'd spent several days sitting at the bedside of his wounded daughter. She was just four years old and had shrapnel wounds to her little chest that was now wrapped in white cloth. Her eyes were closed and I saw her chest rise and fall as she took in breaths of air. A copy of the Quran was close by. Ibrahim sat there quietly, praying for the life of his daughter, and hoping that she would pull through. A bomb had landed on his home and already killed his wife, his son, and his eldest daughter. This child was now all he had.

Despite the personal turmoil he must have been feeling, he didn't seem to hold any anger, which was a rarity in the region at that time. He would have been in his fifties and must have seen a fair bit of loss and terror, but he chose his words carefully and spoke calmly to me as he tried to sum up his feelings. He told me that all he wanted was for his daughter to survive and grow up in a Gaza that had its own borders, its own airports, and its own industries. Far removed from what it was then.

•

The next day, 17 July 2014, most of Australia was asleep when news broke about a missing plane in eastern Ukraine. Malaysian Airlines flight MH17 had disappeared somewhere east of the country's second city, Donetsk, where I'd already spent several weeks that year reporting on a civil war that was raging between the Ukrainian military and Russian-backed separatists.

I watched the news unfold on Twitter and various news wires from my hotel desk in Gaza. Planes don't just go missing, so we assumed it had crashed. Also, the passenger liner was on its way to Kuala Lumpur from Amsterdam and so it was highly likely Australians would be on board. Very soon it became clear that neither mechanical malfunction nor a heavy storm had brought it down. MH17 had flown over a war zone and had been shot out of the sky. It was big news, and unbelievably tragic.

Because my 'beat' was the Middle East, Africa and Europe, Ukraine was part of the territory I was expected to cover and report from. Channel Nine's London-based producer, Eliza Berkery, and I only ever woke up our boss, Channel Nine's Director of News and Current Affairs, Darren Wick, when big news broke overnight, and this was one of those times. Even though the 2014 Gaza war still needed continued coverage, aside from a crew from the ABC, I was the only Australian journalist on the Gaza Strip. During a brief conversation with Wickie it was decided that Luke and I should head to Ukraine to cover the MH17 story immediately. Even though it was on my turf, I was also geographically closer to eastern Ukraine than any of the network's other journalists. It made sense for us to travel back to Tel Aviv, and then fly to Donetsk.

Luke and I started packing our bags, but as we were preparing to walk out of the hotel doors, the Israeli Defence Force made a stunning announcement – it was invading Gaza. Israel had been unable to contain the missiles that were launched from within the Strip, so it was marching in with its heavy artillery. For several days beforehand, thousands of Israeli soldiers had been massing at the border and preparing to cross on foot and in tanks. We had wondered whether it was just an act of provocation designed to scare Hamas militants, or if the Israelis actually meant business. Now we knew.

This was also very big news but the decision about which story to cover was taken out of my hands. The border between Gaza and Israel was now closed and wouldn't be reopened for days, if not weeks. Luke and I were stuck in Gaza, and in for the long haul. I felt torn. I wanted to cover the plane crash because I knew the region and its players so well, but I also wanted to stay in Gaza for the same reason. But ultimately, reporting on conflict is my preference. It also irritates me when I can't see a story through. The adrenaline rush that comes with war reporting can be quite addictive. (Winston Churchill once said that nothing in life is as exhilarating as being shot at without a result. I can certainly relate to that after two bullets narrowly missed me while reporting in Libya in 2011.) I never took unnecessary risks – and of course the story was never about me – but I always felt a certain excitement whenever I stepped into a theatre of war.

Israel's ground invasion was a sharp escalation in the crisis. Peace talks had sputtered along but it was clear that no one had been serious about stopping the rockets. Hamas wanted restrictions relaxed, while Israel wanted to destroy Gaza's network of tunnels. The night following Israel's announcement was bloody and brutal, and all I heard was the long, sustained volley of rockets that launched and exploded minute after minute.

I watched from my hotel room as Mark Regev, an Australian-born diplomat who had become an Israeli government spokesperson, said from Jerusalem, 'The only reason we are going in is because Hamas has rejected the ceasefire proposals; proposals that have been supported by the Arab League and the United Nations. Hamas said no to the ceasefire and now Hamas will pay the price.' The ceasefire which was 'rejected' by Hamas was brokered between Egypt and Israel.

The Israeli Prime Minister Benjamin Netanyahu also spoke up, 'In the face of such extremism, in the face of such violence, in the face of such terror – Israel has no choice but to defend itself.'

American President Barack Obama's relationship with Netanyahu was strained at the time. Obama had categorically supported Israel during its war against Hamas two years prior but his manner had since shifted. The wording was different. All he could say this time was that he hoped Israel's incursion was done in a way that minimised civilian casualties.

The next morning, I received a frantic phone call from Ameera, who had thankfully resumed work with us. Almost breathless, she said, 'Peter, it's been a very bad night. I haven't slept at all. The Israelis were bombing and bombing and bombing. There is a suburb called Shejaia in the east that has been destroyed. There are dozens of dead bodies still lying on the street. People were killed as they ran away from their homes. It's a massacre. I need to go home and be with my children so I am sending a friend of mine to drive you around today. His name is Omar and he will look after you. It's okay, you can trust him.'

What was to come was, quite simply, the most confronting and disturbing day of my life.

Omar picked us up and drove us to the main al-Shifa hospital, which was completely overwhelmed. Busloads and carloads of people were being dropped off at the entrance because there was nowhere else for them to go. They were sleeping on the grass outside the hospital or under trees or on any available space they could find. They were lucky though, because they had been able to escape the carnage. Hundreds hadn't and remained trapped under a barrage of shells.

Thousands of other refugees were taken to schools run by the United Nations, where families could eat and sleep and safely ride out the storm together. It wouldn't remain that way. Israeli missiles later hit several of those schools after it was claimed that Hamas militants had hidden weapons and rockets inside the classrooms. It seemed as though the Israeli war machine was doing a terrible job, and its public relations were in bad shape. People around the world were venting their anger towards Israeli Prime Minister Benjamin Netanyahu who would not ease his army attacks. He maintained he was merely responding to Palestinian aggression. How do you justify striking a UN school though?

Back outside the hospital ER, ambulance after ambulance pulled up and dropped off the dead and wounded. Most of the people had suffered horrendous injuries, such as missing limbs, broken bones, severe cuts and wounds. It was a very hot day and doctors were pushing and yelling at one another out of frustration. They were doing their best to maintain control in an environment where it could so easily have slipped away. Resources were absolutely stretched because medical supplies were already low. It was a desperate case of providing attention and resources to only those who could be saved.

I walked around the back of the hospital to see how the morgue was coping. I saw utes pull up and dump dead bodies. Mothers were crying, brothers were wailing, it was an awfully sad sight. It's religious custom for those of the

Muslim faith to be buried on the same day of their death and family members were doing their best to make sure that was happening. The bodies were loaded into freezers until they could be identified. Then they were wrapped in a white blanket, picked up, and taken to a funeral. But it was a day of extraordinary circumstance. There was hardly any more room inside the morgue, so bodies were left in the open. Piles of dead children lay on the bloodstained floor.

The damage was so severe that we heard a ceasefire had been agreed between Israeli and Palestinian authorities. A temporary two-hour break in fighting to allow paramedics to get into Shejaia and pick up the dead bodies or rescue any remaining survivors. Rumours about ceasefires swirled all the time but no one really took any notice of them. They were always flimsy at best because both sides had such itchy trigger fingers. But this felt different.

I agreed with Luke and Omar that we would go and at least check out things in Shejaia. Jackets and helmets on. It was a fifteen-minute drive to the densely packed eastern suburbs of Gaza, which had been completely destroyed by war. The streets were flattened and huge columns of black smoke rose from several areas. Paramedics were rushing from house to house pulling dead bodies out from underneath the rubble. I walked past dozens of bodies. One elderly lady, whose clamped hands dangled off the stretcher, had died with a look of fear in her eyes.

Half-a-dozen drones circled the sky above. A swarm of them buzzing away. Usually the drones flew in singular fashion, so this group was even more noticeable. They were louder than usual too, because they were lower. The BBC filmed armed fighters dashing around the neighbourhood, so it was assumed that the suburb had been so viciously attacked because Hamas militants were based there.

Luke filmed as fast as he could to try and capture the madness and devastation. Burnt shells of cars, crushed homes and mosques, collapsed trees and powerlines on the ground. It was apocalyptic. I felt incredibly uneasy, so after about fifteen minutes we sped out of there. Not even ten minutes after we escaped, the ceasefire collapsed, and the death toll continued to climb.

The arithmetic of death was about 20:1 – twenty dead Palestinians to one Israeli. But civilians in Gaza made up about 75 per cent of the victims. That was a staggering amount. It's no wonder rage bubbled to the surface.

After seeing the devastation in Shejaia, I thought surely the war would stop. Someone would talk some sense and end the bloodshed, or at least try. But it didn't work like that. Pain and divisions ran too deep. The tough talk continued from Jerusalem, and an equally defiant tone reverberated on the Strip. Suspecting I might hear some more peaceful discussion, I went to a mosque and listened to an imam lead prayers, which were translated to me by Omar. 'Our house has been destroyed and our children have been killed,' the imam said as he encouraged the resistance to fight on.

•

It's always nice to get fan mail, and these were some of the lovely notes I received while reporting in Gaza during the fifty-day war in 2014.

You son of a bitch.

Let's hope Hamas hunts you down.

You are a cretin.

Next time the rocket will land on you, hopefully.

You will end up being dragged around the streets tied to a motorbike until you die.

You may not survive.

The messages were delivered to me via Twitter, after I'd observed that a rocket had been fired from a compound across the road from my hotel and was on its way to Israel. It wasn't an aggressive post, it was just something that I witnessed, and in the interests of balance I perhaps naively reported it. The threats continued for hours.

Someone giving deadly information to enemy while a guest of Gaza is not a journalist but a spy. Spies get shot.

Filthy Zionist pet dog.

Kick this man out of Gaza.

The irony was that I'd been in Gaza for weeks and had covered the lopsided scale of Palestinian death and destruction caused by Israel's military might. In any case, I got the message.

I'd never received any death threats before, and when someone says you should die, you tend to take notice.

I took the messages seriously, and began to feel as though Luke and I might be even less safe than we already were. We had been working twenty-hour days in a heated and violent atmosphere. Without proper sleep and rest, my mind began to play tricks on me. One evening I was on the balcony of the hotel, in between live crosses to Channel Nine, when I thought I saw a missile heading right for Luke and me. I fell to the ground and raised my voice as if to say *Look out!* Nothing happened. Luke looked at me and laughed. The missile I'd seen was a white bird flapping its wings as it gracefully flew through the air from the ocean to the hotel. I shook my head. I was going bonkers. Luke continued to laugh, and then I laughed too. But Luke also told me he knew exactly what I thought and felt because the same thing had happened to him a day or two earlier. It was definitely time to go.

It might seem like it would be a great joy or relief to leave dangerous, war-torn places, but it's actually not such an easy thing to do. I would not be human if I didn't feel the fear that people experienced, the desperation of living in extraordinarily difficult and dangerous environments, the struggle of sourcing clean water and food, or finding an hour of peaceful sleep. So when I say goodbye to new friends like Ameera who have put themselves in harm's way to keep me alive, it's hard to just drop it all at the airport. I can leave, they cannot. I live in a country where I am free to do and say what I like, when I like, but they aren't. For example, all Ameera's husband wanted to do was visit Jerusalem and pray, but he couldn't even do that.

I left Gaza and Israel with a heavy heart, while the local people stayed behind and picked up the pieces, knowing it was highly likely war would resume again, probably in the not-too-distant future.

Chapter 2

THE PEOPLE WANT THE FALL OF THE REGIME

THE LIBYAN UPRISING

In 2011 Libya was a powder keg about to explode. But allow me to back things up for a bit of character development before I tell you what happened when the wick was lit.

Originally I wanted to call this book *An Idiot Abroad*. Unfortunately for me, Ricky Gervais had beaten me to the punch with his British TV comedy show. Shame, because it was a perfectly apt description of my partnership with cameraman James Gillings. In fact, we used to call ourselves 'the idiots abroad' as a kind of self-deprecating humour whenever things became too dangerous. I was from Cairns, he was from Coffs Harbour: two small-town lads who often found ourselves in the strangest of situations, such as travelling to places everyone else was running away from, and having a quiet chuckle about it.

James and I got on well. We made decisions together. But at times I wanted to kill him. Other times, he wanted to kill me. It was a healthy relationship. Also, I never made a decision without consulting James. If he was uncomfortable with a situation or direction we were heading, I wouldn't go. That was a rule we established early in our partnership.

After the Libyan uprising first erupted on 17 February 2011, we were among the first Western journalists to cross into the country from Egypt.

For forty-two years Libya had been under the rule of Colonel Muammar Gaddafi. Born in a desert tent on the outskirts of Sirte, a coastal Libyan city, Gaddafi was a passionate Arab nationalist who rose to power in 1969. As a charismatic and handsome 27-year-old army captain, he led a bloodless coup against King Idris who had turned Libya into a constitutional monarchy following its independence from Italian colonial rule eighteen years prior.

Gaddafi thought Libya was too closely aligned with the West so he removed American and British military bases, expelled Italian and Jewish Libyans, and took control of foreign-owned oil fields, making him one of the richest men on the planet. He called himself Africa's King of Kings and his ambition was to unite the Arab world. Traditional Islamic laws, such as the prohibition of alcohol and gambling, were reinstated. But as the years passed, Gaddafi's behaviour became erratic and unpredictable. His hatred of the West burned him up and his government started financing terrorist organisations around the world.

During the 1980s the West blamed him for numerous terrorist attacks in Europe, including the bombing of an airliner over Lockerbie in Scotland that killed 270 people, and the bombing of a West German dance hall. US President Ronald Reagan, who nicknamed Gaddafi the 'mad dog of the Middle East', bombed Tripoli in retaliation – an attack in which the colonel was injured and his infant daughter was killed.

It wasn't until the late 1990s, after Gaddafi turned over alleged perpetrators of the Lockerbie bombing to international authorities, that his image abroad improved and his country gradually returned to the global community. He was brought in from the cold.

Within Libya, Gaddafi's 42-year leadership was powerful and ruthless. His regime was built on fear and intimidation, but by 2011 it was starting to fray. You push people around for too long, eventually they retaliate.

Disaffected Libyan youths watched during the so-called Arab Spring as Tunisians, and then Egyptians, booted out their governments. The young Libyans wanted the same thing: a new and free life that their parents weren't ever able to have.

So protesters who were sick and tired of poor living conditions and government corruption organised a 'day of rage' in several Libyan cities. Day of rage was right.

Like Egypt, and many other Muslim nations for that matter, public dissent was not tolerated in Gaddafi's Libya. Loud and critical voices were seen as destabilising to the regime and so it came down hard on the perpetrators – the response was swift and brutal.

Protests led to fighting and it got uglier by the minute. I'd only really just returned to London following the Egyptian uprising, and started making plans to return to the region as the uprising grew and the pictures became more violent. Government forces knew full well what had happened in Egypt and Tunisia and obviously felt that silencing the voices wasn't enough; the momentum needed to be stopped before it was too late. Dozens of protesters were massacred by Gaddafi's elite security soldiers who fired live ammunition from rooftops and helicopters into crowds of people below. Bodies were everywhere. It was a fresh hell. A heavy response like that usually worked. Death, or the threat of it, scares people enough to maintain order. Not this time.

The tide of anger and resentment only grew and grew. It seemed as though the more people died, the angrier the rest of the freedom movement became. A day of rage became a week of rage. That fuse on the powder keg had been ignited and there was no turning back.

Government buildings were torched and the police and army withdrew. If any Gaddafi loyalists were found they were either shot or lynched by an angry mob. Many government supporters switched sides and joined the revolution. By the time we were at the border, trying to get in, the uprising had gone further than anyone could have imagined.

•

It was just James and me at Egypt's border with Libya. No translator. No security guard. No help at all. All we had was basic broadcasting gear, a little spare clothing, and a couple of hundred bucks. It was going to go well.

The border was a shambles. A storm of chaos and confusion. Media and medical workers were trying to get in while thousands of Libyan refugees – many of them from other African nations who worked in Libya's oil ports – were trying to get out. People were rushing and shouting, and tempers were boiling over.

Dealing with Egyptian authorities in these circumstances was worse than a pain in the arse and we were going nowhere. I understood they were paranoid and aggressive because there was a war going on and the language barrier was a significant hurdle to try and overcome. I didn't speak a word of Arabic, and the people I was trying to reason with didn't speak a word of English. Two brick walls standing next to each other would have had the same result.

After several failed attempts at haggling and pleading with the Egyptian officials, I saw a TV crew from Denmark who appeared to be having some success. So James and I kind of just joined them. They felt sorry for us, I think, so they helped us get stamped out and we were soon on our way. Thank you, Denmark. I will always have a soft spot for you and not just because you have lovely ice-creams.

James and I walked across the frontier, which in this case was a huge bitumen road separated by two concrete walls on either side. Remarkably, the Libyan end was staffed by a young bloke sitting on a chair with an AK-47 for company. That was it. He was a picture of complete calm and it was quite comical after the bedlam we'd just passed a few hundred metres back. There was no border control. No one to stamp your passport. We were effectively illegal immigrants in a country at war.

In this north-eastern region of Libya, Gaddafi's government troops had been chased off and it was a free-for-all. There were no quizzical looks as film crews approached. The rebels may not have had the firepower to match Gaddafi yet, especially in the air, but they had something that was arguably more important – the media. We could broadcast their voices and struggles to the world. So we were generally welcomed and looked after.

The 'border guard' whistled and then waved to one of his friends in the distance and motioned for him to bring a car. I didn't even have to ask. 'He will take you to Tobruk,' the kid said. Deal done. No questions asked. After the struggles on the Egyptian side, the Libyan part was easy. But we were heading into a conflict so it was a whole lot riskier.

I had no idea who this driver was or who he was even aligned with. Was it beyond the realms of possibility that we could be picked up by a Gaddafi loyalist who would kidnap us and use us as pawns? Maybe it was. Maybe it wasn't.

So there I was, strapped into the back seat of a rusty old sedan while James was in the front passenger seat. The driver was tearing down the motorway doing about 120 kilometres an hour when we drove right into a sandstorm.

I'd been in hailstorms and snowstorms but a sandstorm was a new experience. I could barely see a metre in front of the car as it tore down the motorway with an ineffective and squeaky windscreen wiper. It didn't slow the driver down. I held the door so hard that my knuckles turned white. I was waiting for the moment of impact when our car ploughed into a home, or a roadblock. Game over.

I tugged on James's shirt to see if he was feeling the same but there was no response. I pulled harder. No response. I leaned forward and saw that he was fast asleep! Body relaxed, mouth open, catching z's completely oblivious to the dangerous situation I was sure we were in! Are you kidding me?

We'd gone days without sleep just to get to the border so Jimmy was buggered and had stolen a moment to rest. It's funny now but at the time it wasn't. Anyway, we were on our way into war-torn Libya. Destination Tobruk.

•

Tobruk holds an important place in Australian history. The stories of our troops' experiences there in World War II are legendary.

Back in 1941, Australian diggers were part of an Allied campaign in Libya against Italian and German forces that had Egypt in their sights. For eight months, our men bunkered down in the port city of Tobruk, a strategically important harbour for both sides. As well as withstanding daily bombings, tank attacks, and artillery barrages by the

Germans and Italians, the diggers battled extreme elements, from the desert's searing heat to its bitterly cold nights. They hid in caves and crevices, and dug tunnels and shelters to protect themselves from the mighty Middle Eastern sandstorms, but also to help fend off a formidable opponent led by the so-called Desert Fox – German commander Erwin Rommel. The Australians were known as 'the rats of Tobruk', a nickname that was meant to be derogatory but became a badge of honour when the campaign was successful.

Seventy years after our brave 'rats' fought there, war had returned to Tobruk. It was the first Libyan city to be liberated from Gaddafi's government troops. Although, in reality, the liberation was more a result of government soldiers deserting the army and joining the revolution. According to Gaddafi, the 'rats' were back. But this time it was the demonstrators and the media who were the vermin. He said the rats and cockroaches were like germs and enemies of Libya who deserved to die. He swore he would fight to the last drop of his blood.

By the time we arrived in Tobruk, a few hours after we'd crossed the Egyptian border, the fighting was over and the city bore scars of the recent violent uprising. In the main 'Freedom Square', the police station had been torched and burnt to a black shell, a symbol of the end of Gaddafi's rule in Tobruk.

There was a feeling of euphoria in the city as people waved the old Libyan flag – the tricolours of green, red and black – which had been outlawed by Gaddafi. Residents raised their weapons in victory and shot celebratory gunfire into the air. This was a common reaction whenever victories were declared in Libya, but it was a cause of great frustration to James and me because what goes up must come down and bullets needed to land somewhere.

Our stay in Tobruk was short, however, as the frontlines of the civil war rapidly shifted west. The rebels had momentum, cities were tumbling like dominoes, and we needed to keep up. So James and I hitched a ride towards Benghazi – ground zero for Libya's revolution. The eastern city was where the civil war had begun on 17 February when security forces opened fire on protesters, and it was still central to the war.

We were driven by another young fella who took us 300 kilometres west to the city of al-Bayda. He didn't ask for any money but told us it was as far as he could go. We were, in effect, hitchhiking across a war zone. At al-Bayda we were questioned by a few dozen local elders, an example of the kind of shotgun governments that seemed to be in charge throughout the country.

For more than an hour, James and I sat in a stuffy room as the men discussed our movements. 'What are you doing here?' they asked. Mercenaries from Chad and Niger had been caught a few days before. Snipers who were paid by the Gaddafi regime to shoot protesters and journalists. The elders showed us video footage of ordinary Libyans marching down main streets who were picked off at random by snipers. Up to 10,000 dollars per kill was the reported payment they received. Cold-blooded killers in high-rises.

The mood was incredibly tense. James and I thought we might be in trouble because they wouldn't let us go. They were speaking Arabic, which certainly didn't ease our concerns. It's a beautiful language but when it's spoken aggressively it can be a bit unnerving to an untrained ear. Did they think we were spies? we wondered.

More time passed before they finally released us. 'Welcome to Libya,' they said. 'You want to go to Benghazi?' they asked. 'Yes please,' we replied. Not a moment later another young man was summonsed to pick us up and drive us the rest of the way – another 250 kilometres – to the country's second largest city. This man drove with an AK-47 on his lap, which made the journey a little more frightening. My eyes darted from the road to the gun and back again. At that time in Libya, there were no road rules. The people drove as fast as they wanted; often it seemed on whatever lane they wanted. So this was another nervy ride down a major highway and, yes, James fell asleep again.

●

James and I made it to Benghazi about a week after the 17 February uprising that had begun the revolution. Unlike in Bahrain and Iran, where similar uprisings in 2011 were quashed early, in Libya it seemed that the resistance might just have a chance. Prisoners had escaped from jail, and Gaddafi's lavish compounds in the east of the country had been overrun. We saw ordinary Libyan children swimming and laughing in the dictator's opulent swimming pools. Police stations and military bases had been invaded and weapons storage facilities had been ransacked, so anyone and everyone was armed. Libya was completely lawless.

James and I had been covering the January and February anti-government protests in Egypt, so we had an idea of what to expect, but the Libyan revolution was an entirely different ball game. Gaddafi had no interest in ceding power and was willing to do anything to keep it, or at least present an image of being in control. He'd just delivered his defiant and now infamous '*zenga zenga* [street by street]' speech from the balcony of his compound in Tripoli.

'I am calling upon the millions from one end of the deserts to the other. We will march in our millions to purify Libya. Inch by inch, house by house, street by street, person by person until the country is clean of the dirt and impurities,' he shouted with his fists clenched.

Gaddafi accused the protesters of being high on drugs and drunk on alcohol and said they were being influenced by foreign governments who were after the nation's rich oil reserves. He told his followers there was a conspiracy to control Libyan oil and land, and to colonise Libya again.

The problem for Gaddafi, however, was that his closest aides were deserting him. It became a huge turning point in the war.

Embassies were shutting down and civilians were being evacuated. Australian consular officials offered a way out for the few Australian journalists who were there, including James and me and my mate Mike Amor, who is an excellent correspondent from Channel Seven. The consular invitation was appreciated but declined because history was unfolding before our eyes.

Alarmed at the crisis we were in, our bosses back in Sydney sent a security consultant, Shaun Filer, to help us. Thankfully, Shaun came with a bit of cash to get us around and he was also trained in medical trauma so if we got hurt he was a good man to have close by. While James and I worked, Shaun would scan the people and the places, keeping a lookout for trouble. He also organised a wonderful and kind-hearted driver, Mousa, and a translator named Osama, who preferred to be called Sam. Our team of two was now a team of five.

Muammar Gaddafi's forty-year grip on power was weakening by the day as freedom fighters in the country's east, and pockets of resistance in the west, set their sights on the capital, Tripoli.

But, unlike Tunisia and Egypt, it would not be a quick revolution. Despite the growing protest movement and the desertions of his aides, Colonel Gaddafi still had some support and, most importantly, control of the military.

There was another big reason why it would take months, if at all, for the protesters to unseat Gaddafi from power – the rebel army wasn't very good. While they had plenty of anger and determination, they lacked co-ordination and skill. They were an untrained civilian army of teachers, students, doctors, lawyers, and oil workers going up against a powerful military machine.

I spoke to a former major of Gaddafi's army who had defected to the rebels. He told me he expected Libya to fall. What he could not tell me was how or when.

For weeks, our little team followed the rebel advance as they made small gains in the east. We commuted every day from our hotel in Benghazi to rebel positions in Ajdabiya, al-Brega, and Ras Lanuf. We spent hours and hours driving daily to different positions, through more sandstorms, talking to different fighters and commanders. 'Today we will kill Gaddafi,' they said assuredly. 'Tomorrow we will invade Tripoli!' others would say. But hope was one thing, reality something else. Despite their enthusiasm, their inexperienced civilian army would not trouble Gaddafi or his military machine. They wouldn't get anywhere near Tripoli. At times I wondered if they truly thought they could.

I attended a few training camps where senior soldiers taught young men how to fire a gun. Not an automatic rifle, but a handgun. It took time to get the hang of it and no one blamed them for being slow to learn. Just weeks earlier they'd been living completely different lives, often as doctors or students; now they were stepping into a theatre of war and fighting for a future. I saw hope in their eyes, but there was also doubt, a doubt that stemmed from fear. They knew what they were up against.

Gaddafi's troops were experienced and deadly. Because they were under the command of Gaddafi and his equally fearsome sons, the troops were highly trained – they learned how to torture, how to maim, and how to kill. The colonel was ruthless and demanded his soldiers and pilots take out their own countrymen. If they failed, their own families were placed at risk. More importantly, Gaddafi had something the rebels didn't: military aircraft. The playing field was lopsided because of his army's jets.

When I looked at the rebel army, I often wondered if I was staring at men and boys who would soon be dead on a battlefield while their mothers would be at home crying their hearts out.

More than a few particular encounters with the rebels convinced me that their attempts to overthrow Colonel Gaddafi would take time.

Once, we were stopped at a checkpoint near al-Brega and a rebel with an overblown ego leaned into our car and presented a grenade to us. It sat in his hand just in front of Mousa, our driver. The pin was still attached. We shouted at him to get away. He just looked at us and laughed and then walked away.

At other times we would be close to the frontlines when Gaddafi's forces would push back. Rather than stay and fight, and hold defensive positions, rebel soldiers would shit themselves, jump in their cars, and leave their units. As soon as they regrouped they'd creep back to where they were in what became a long game of highway ping-pong between government and rebel forces.

Misinformation was another frustrating issue. One time we were bunkered down in a hotel in the small town of Ajdabiya, about 200 kilometres south of Benghazi. I remember it well because I had one of the all-time great lamb shawarmas – sort of like a kebab but with less salad. Good food was understandably hard to get at the time. There wasn't much in the way of hotel workers either, so rooms could be rented, but they were usually dirty and unkempt from a heavy stream of journalists who had drifted in and out. It was like we were all squatting but still paying a pretty penny.

We were trying to file a story for the evening news bulletin when panicked word came through that the eastern frontline just a few kilometres away from us had been breached by Gaddafi's tanks and troops. We hurriedly grabbed what few things we had, threw a few hundred American dollars at the front desk, jumped in our van, and took off back to Benghazi. Hours later, we were told that nothing of the sort had happened. No lines had been broken. The region was on edge, which caused fear and rumour to spread quickly. Fear was contagious and everyone at one point or another felt it.

Weeks into the war, we finally made it to the frontline of Libya's eastern resistance. The rebels' ragtag army, made up of fighters, army deserters, and ordinary citizens, had already suffered tremendously. Thousands had been killed and many more had gone missing – presumed dead – but it was too late for the nation's restless youth to turn back.

We were in a place called Ras Lanuf, a tiny seaside port town positioned right in the middle of Libya's northern coastline. It was as far as the rebels could advance. The next major township west along the desert highway was Sirte, the birthplace and tribal home of Gaddafi, and a major pro-government stronghold. Getting anywhere near Sirte was a certified death sentence for a Westerner. Ras Lanuf was where east met west and was home to roughly 10,000 Libyans but it was strategically important for one reason – it had oil. In Libya at the time, oil was worth more than gold.

I was filming a piece to camera with James for the evening news, while Shaun, Mousa and Sam kept watch. I was standing just behind the rebel position, where groups of rebels were casually gathered with assault rifles in what was one of those lulls between fighting. Dead quiet. I explained to the camera how important Ras Lanuf was for the rebels to hold, but it would be difficult because their 'hold' was flimsy at best. There weren't that many fighters on the ground and it seemed to me they would be easily overrun in the face of a strong counter-offensive.

Sure enough, there was a rumble in the distance and the rebels near us panicked. I looked around as dozens of young men quickly packed up and raced to their cars. Many of them piled into rusted sedans while others climbed into Toyota HiLuxs and burned back towards the east.

Our driver had jumped into our van, but it was facing the wrong way on a single-lane highway. We were losing precious seconds as he turned it around. Rebel vehicles were kicking up brown dust as accelerators were floored and vehicles raced back towards the relative safety of larger towns much further east.

Rebels shouted at us in Arabic, 'Get out of here! Gaddafi is coming. Gaddafi is coming!' Gaddafi himself wasn't really coming, but his name was often used as a collective term for his forces, which were in truth an extension of him. It was still the early stages of the uprising and so a no-fly zone was yet to be imposed by NATO. Gaddafi's military jets were on the loose and under strict orders to attack. The thought of the jets was what unsettled me the most.

We finally got the van heading east. It was a slow ride, or at least it felt that way. James filmed from inside our white nine-seater as rebel vehicles overtook us. I watched as a ute tore past us with a large anti-aircraft gun attached to its tray. It was a common sight. What wasn't common was the rebel who stood behind the weapon of the moving HiLux. He had military fatigues on, dark glasses, and a chequered scarf wrapped around his face to protect his lungs from the dust. It looked like something straight out of *Mad Max*.

Our vehicles were moving at speeds well above a hundred kilometres an hour but the rumble behind was getting louder. The jets were closing in. Then came the gunfire.

TUT-TUT-TUT-TUT-TUT-TUT-TUT from the speeding HiLux as the soldier squeezed the trigger. He looked like he was in his early twenties and he pumped round after round from his heavy weapon, which was aimed skywards.

The rumble was on top of us, as engines roared loudly. I looked at Shaun, and he looked at me. Nothing was said but I assumed we felt the same thing. We were waiting for the bomb to hit. If it struck, at least it would be quick.

TUT-TUT-TUT-TUT-TUT-TUT. The firing continued as our van and a convoy of several other vehicles sped away. Outside the van's window to my left were the crystal blue waters of the Mediterranean Sea. To my right were the dry, dusty golden sands of the Sahara desert. Beautiful contrasting colours in a nerve-racking dash for safety. The van was hot and I was sweating. I could see the jet out the right-hand side window, and a second later a huge plume of black and brown sand shot skywards from an open farming field. The bomb had been dropped, but its target was unclear. 'Whoa!' I shouted as I stared with a mixture of fear and wonder.

The jet screamed past us, but amazingly our motorcade hadn't been hit. A short time later we arrived at a checkpoint where other vehicles had stopped. The jet had gone, but where? No one could answer. It had vanished from view but the mood was still incredibly tense. The jets would regularly disappear only to reappear seconds later.

As we caught our breaths a few laughing soldiers ran towards us with the news. The planes, or at least one of them, had been shot out of the sky. 'We saw the crashed jet and the dead pilots inside them,' they said. *'Allahu Akbar. Allahu Akbar!'* their listeners cheered. It was a small victory, but a victory nonetheless.

The rebel soldiers passed food and fruit juice around in celebration. I didn't go to the crash site, as I was a bit shaken. Channel Nine's contracted news affiliates such as Reuters would film that for us. Sometimes it wasn't worth putting ourselves in unnecessary danger because we would get the vision anyway. But as we made the long drive back to our hotel that afternoon I wondered, had the plane really been struck? Or had the pilot grown sick of killing his own people and ditched it? It was the kind of question that Gaddafi's oppressive regime made you consider.

•

The nature of the modern news business is that, after a while, without major developments the stories from one place start to look the same. They lose their punch and affect the viewers less and less, meaning an inevitable slide down the news agenda. It's at about this point that we get the call from the news director. Kind of like the football coach waving from the sideline for his players to come off the field. 'You've had enough for now, son. Well played. Come and have a rest.'

So in March 2011 we packed our bags and drove for seventeen hours non-stop in the back of a cramped van back to Cairo. But it wasn't the end of our time in Libya. We'd be back again and again.

Not long after we left, an international coalition led by French President Nicolas Sarkozy, and backed up by the British Prime Minister David Cameron and the American

President Barack Obama, intervened in the Libyan civil war. They weren't interested in sending boots on the ground, but don't be fooled by the rhetoric. While armies didn't necessarily invade, there were specialists and advisors in the country who helped to train the rebel movement.

The allied leaders pushed to send warplanes into the region and bomb Gaddafi targets such as compounds, weapons facilities, and potential hideouts. The argument was that this would provide suitable cover for the rebel army on the ground – it was their fight after all – while also reducing the chance of allied casualties to a minimum, meaning less blowback on the political leaders.

The balance of power started to shift. NATO imposed a no-fly zone, grounding Gaddafi's jets, which evened up the playing field. But Gaddafi's forces were still much stronger, and armed a hell of a lot better. His army still had the tanks, and more sophisticated weaponry. So skirmishes between rebels and government forces continued for months over the same stretches of land and sand.

The death toll climbed and more of Libya's sons and daughters were buried. It's an uneasy feeling watching people bury their dead while also scanning the horizon for attackers. I felt this mood in Gaza too, where the threat of aerial assaults was always real – especially where masses of people were gathered.

Try as they might, even after months of training, rebel fighters in the country's east just could not break past the city of Sirte – Gaddafi's well-fortified ancestral home. It was looking like the civil war would end in a stalemate. There were even serious suggestions that the country would have to split in two, and Benghazi would become the capital of Eastern Libya.

But while all the attention was on the resistance in the east, the real game changer came from the west. After more of Gaddafi's advisors fled the country or defected, rebel armies on the other side of Sirte made quiet gains. Fighters from the so-called Zintan and Misrata brigades inched closer and closer to the capital, Tripoli.

In August 2011, rebel fighters made a surprising and lightning advance into the capital. The remaining government troops were caught on the hop and bailed. Gaddafi and his family fled. Opposition forces stormed key sites and, six months after the protests in Benghazi that had sparked the civil war, the rebel army finally won the battle for liberty.

James and I were in London as the rebels made that lightning advance on Tripoli from the west, so we packed our bags and immediately headed for the Libyan capital. But flying was a no-go because the airport at Tripoli had been destroyed in the fighting and most passenger planes had been set on fire.

We flew instead to Tunisia, and then drove to its border with Libya at Dehiba because the main western crossing at Ras Ajdir was too unsafe. Once in Libya, we travelled through barren country, past vast mountain ranges and small villages before we arrived in Zintan after more than a day of travelling. On the way to Tripoli, we slept in some very odd places, such as an old disused post office. Getting help was difficult during the day because it was the holy month of Ramadan, which meant Libyans were fasting during the daylight hours. If we were hungry we ate away from the Libyans as a matter of courtesy. On the plus side, most of the fighters slept during the day so it didn't feel as dangerous. But one day, as I was waiting for a car to pick me up, a bullet sped past my ear. A hot flash and a sharp zip and it burrowed into the bitumen at my feet. That suggested it had been fired into the air as a form of celebration some kilometres away, proving, as James and I always feared, that what went up, came down.

•

When we arrived in Tripoli, I walked amongst the ruins of the infamous Abu Salim prison, which had been one of the most notorious jails in the world. No place in Libya summed up Colonel Gaddafi's cruelty quite like it. It was where those who opposed or threatened his rule were locked up, often without trial.

Political prisoners were treated worse than murderers and rapists because they had the potential to destabilise Gaddafi's regime. So they were locked up in isolated sections of the prison. It wasn't just their bodies that were incarcerated but, more importantly, their minds. Once they were brought to the prison, they felt as though they didn't exist anymore.

I saw the dark, cold rooms where men were beaten and tortured while they were interrogated by burly guards.

Prisoners were struck with rods and steel bars, whipped with cables and electrical wires, and attacked by dogs that were trained to bite them. Sometimes there wasn't even a reason for punishment to be handed out; it was done for fun.

A few days earlier, when the rebel fighters arrived in Tripoli, they had stormed Abu Salim, fired their weapons at security officers, and flung open the gates of hell. I was told that the guards at Abu Salim had retreated after a short gun battle, while the inmates cheered loudly. Large steel doors were unlocked and metal gates swung open as prisoners tasted freedom for the first time in years. Imagine the sight as they strode out of their blocks and escaped. Some of the prisoners had been stuck in the jail for decades with no word from their families outside. In an instant, everything changed.

I sat in one of the cells, which was a few metres square in size, and was lit by one light bulb. I was told that twelve people had lived there, crammed in side by side, all sleeping on flat foam mattresses. Sheets had been tossed around the room and there were sketches on the walls. Some prisoners had scratched dates and Arabic writing onto the white concrete, wondering if they would ever be released.

I noticed loudspeakers near the roof of the hall. Pro-Gaddafi political songs and speeches had been played loudly at all hours of the day and night, causing the prisoners great aggravation and many sleepless nights.

The most haunting feeling came from a concrete yard where more than 1200 prisoners were massacred in 1996.

Stories vary but according to Human Rights Watch a prison riot erupted on the morning of 28 June 1996. Two guards were delivering breakfast to the cells but when they opened the door, inmates grabbed their keys and took the guards hostage. Libya's top security official, Abdullah Senussi, who was married to the sister of Muammar Gaddafi's wife, rushed in to speak to a delegation of four prisoners who represented the rioters. The prisoners wanted improved conditions such as better food, beds, and baths. They were also tired of being degraded and insulted. Senussi said he would address their concerns once all the prisoners returned to their cells and the hostages were released.

The next morning the inmates were lured into the courtyard, which was surrounded by high walls. Standing on top of the walls were armed guards holding AK-47s. The prisoners were trapped. A grenade was thrown in and the killing frenzy began. Over the next few hours, guards fired at anything that moved until everyone was dead. The next day the rotting bodies were placed on wheelbarrows and tossed into trenches. These mass graves were eventually covered in concrete.

The families of the victims went years without even knowing whether their son, brother or father had been murdered. Details remained scarce until almost ten years later, in 2006, when the massacre was confirmed by Gaddafi because he said the families had a right to know. Death was what you got for criticising the regime. Most people suspected it was Gaddafi who ordered the massacre at Abu Salim.

•

A few days after my arrival in Tripoli, I was trapped in an elevator on the seventeenth floor of my hotel with the legendary war correspondent Marie Colvin. Marie wore a black eye patch over her left eye following an incident while reporting in Sri Lanka several years earlier. Sporadic gunfire had continued in Tripoli for days after its fall as isolated clashes broke out, which often led to power outages. Great. I don't like tight spaces and had no idea how long I would be kept in this small, dark space so high up. And I had a live broadcast for the Channel Nine news to get to!

'If the cables snap and the elevator goes down you've got a better chance of survival if you lie down on your back,' Marie said in an American accent. I never forgot that, purely because it seemed so absurd. A lift plummeting seventeen storeys would surely mean certain death. But I probably would have followed her advice if it meant saving my skin, especially as it came from Colvin, who had a tonne of experience and whose articles I always loved reading. (It was the only conversation I had with Marie, who was sadly killed by a rocket attack while reporting in Syria the following year.)

By then, Tripoli was the Wild West. There was no law and order and it was out of control. An entry poster at the Corinthia Hotel, where journalists from most foreign media outlets were staying, read 'No Guns Allowed'. It seemed everyone was armed. One night, James and I were having dinner at the hotel when a shot was fired from the neighbouring lobby. A guard had accidentally shot his finger off and had left a trail of blood on the marble floor.

Another night I was about to do a live cross to the *Today* show from the hotel balcony when another bullet zipped past my ear. It was travelling so fast that it burned the air as it passed by and sounded like a high-pitched mosquito. It happened in a flash and I could only wonder what would have resulted if it had been a few centimetres closer.

It had been dangerous on our first trip to Libya in February, but now the danger had increased, and so had the price of safety. During that first trip, we were driven around for free. Now it cost at least US$500. Even though rebel soldiers had flooded into the capital, some Gaddafi loyalists were continuing to fight, and we were told that snipers were still hiding in buildings and apartments. No one knew where the colonel was.

I went to Gaddafi's sprawling and once well-fortified Bab al-Aziziya palace. It was a symbol of the luxury he had taken for himself and denied most of his countrymen and women. It had a theme park, wild animals and plenty of gold on show. On the day I visited, it was crawling with the rebel fighters who had chased him out of town. I looked at the happy faces of the people who were now stealing his possessions. But because they were still armed and wildly firing their bullets it was a cause for concern. The flak jackets were on. I saw the huge lounge rooms, the dining areas, the sprawling yards, and then the underground tunnels Gaddafi and his family had used to travel around the city. I climbed down a steel ladder to the first level and walked along them. There were several levels of well-built concrete corridors snaking around the city. Gaddafi used them to travel from his home to any of the hotels he owned so he couldn't be detected at ground level. I assumed they were also how he made his hasty getaway. Inside the tunnels were many rooms, offices, and sleeping quarters. There were even a few discarded golf carts for transport.

Above the tunnel entrance was the famous statue Gaddafi had built in the 1980s of a fist crushing an American jet. It was now covered in graffiti and freedom fighters stood nearby, blasting the sky with celebratory gunfire. It wasn't so long ago that Colonel Gaddafi was standing right there delivering one of his speeches to the nation, trying to inspire his followers and criticise his opponents. I wondered if he was now in a hideout somewhere, looking at the images on television of his beloved fortress falling apart. He must have thought, 'How on earth did that happen?' What happened to the millions of people he claimed loved him?

I stood next to the gold-plated fist statue as heavy machinery was brought in to tear it from the ground. It was then placed on a truck and driven away.

The Libyan people would never have dreamed they could one day walk through Bab al-Aziziya palace. Colonel Gaddafi was a man to be feared. His face was still on show on advertising boards around the city. Pictures of a smiling dictator, dressed in his trademark robes, and clenching his fists, to remind the people who was in charge. But one by one the symbols of his rule were being ripped down.

There was celebration in Tripoli, but it was full of death too. The dying days of the regime had been violent as rebel fighters seized the city.

In one of the city's hospitals, hundreds of dead bodies were found. Doctors had fled as Gaddafi loyalists burst in and fired their weapons at anyone and anything. On a stretcher? Didn't matter. Connected to life support machines? The gunmen didn't care. Patients were gunned down in a bloody and heartless last act of retribution. But it wasn't the only one.

While in Tripoli, I stood in a dark tin shed built from corrugated iron as rays of light streamed through bullet holes that had punctured the sides. I saw human bones on the blackened earth and smelled the sickly stench of death. We were told that up to fifty people who were accused of being anti-government protesters had been locked inside the shed before grenades were thrown in. The shed was then set on fire and blasted with live ammunition. Somehow some of the prisoners managed to escape but they were shot as they fled. It was assumed the massacre, which would qualify as a war crime, was a final act of defiance as the determined rebels closed in on the city.

The shed stood at the end of a long dirt track inside the military base of the infamous Khamis Brigade, the nation's most feared militia which was loyal to Khamis Gaddafi – one of Muammar's sons who may have been an heir apparent.

The brigade's massive headquarters was no longer the seat of fear. Its grey concrete buildings were mostly destroyed by some well-placed NATO bombs. All that really remained was a statue of a large eagle at the entrance. It had lost its prey.

•

Two months later, in October when I was on another assignment in Belfast, news unexpectedly broke that Colonel Gaddafi had been killed. He'd been hiding out in Sirte where the so-called Misrata brigade of rebels encountered strong resistance. So strong they assumed someone important was being protected. They assumed correctly. Colonel Gaddafi was there.

Sensing the defence of his birthplace was not going to stay intact, Gaddafi tried to escape with his sons and bodyguards in a forty-car convoy. But it didn't get far. It was spotted by NATO helicopters and a bomb was dropped to cut off the exit route. Gaddafi had been hit. He wasn't dead but he was badly injured from the shrapnel.

The 70-year-old scurried out of the car and ran off the road, where he hid inside a large concrete pipe. Very quickly, the rebels found their man and surrounded him. They couldn't believe it. They grabbed at him and called him a dog. They treated him as he had treated them. It was primal. 'What did I ever do to you?' he was filmed asking as he begged for his life. In the dictator's delusional world, he appeared to forget that he'd caused misery to hundreds of thousands of people.

Colonel Gaddafi looked a tired old man. Balding and bleeding from the face, he was roughed up as the militia shouted at him and then tried to put him on the back of a Toyota HiLux. The hope would have been to arrest him and try him in a court of law. But the hunters couldn't contain their excitement and there was a chorus of men who screamed '*Allahu Akbar!*' If the pictures are anything to go by, it seems that street justice was always going to be Gaddafi's endgame. One moment the old man was alive, grimacing in pain, the next his dead body was being dragged along the street, a gunshot wound to his head and torso visible. Regardless of who he was, or what he'd done, the mobile phone vision was unpleasant to watch.

Libyans queued for days to see his dead body, which was taken to Misrata and left in a meat freezer before it was buried. It was as if they needed to see it to be sure that he was gone.

Muammar Gaddafi's death provided some closure to many people who had suffered during his ruthless forty-year rule. But Libya's future was as uncertain as ever. The country was lawless and there were no police or military. During my trips to Libya in 2011, just about every person I saw had a weapon: handguns, AK-47 assault rifles, grenades, RPGs, anti-aircraft weaponry. Men were firing guns, kids were carrying them. After Gaddafi's death, the fighters would not hand the weapons back, which did not augur well for the country's future.

Libya was a country of many tribes and local militias, and there was no agreement between them and the nation's political parties on how to move forward. Order couldn't be maintained and the country quickly became a breeding ground for North African jihadis. Libya, once a proud and prosperous nation, was a basket case.

Towards the end of 2014, battle-hardened Libyan Islamists returned from fighting in Iraq and Syria and set about establishing a self-proclaimed caliphate in north Africa. The so-called Islamic State (IS) established a base at Derna – a few hundred kilometres west of Tobruk where James and I had driven through a few years before. They also set up a base in al-Bayda where we had been questioned in 2011 by those elders on the way to Benghazi.

If anyone was found to be 'un-Islamic' they were reportedly stoned, beheaded, and crucified. Rather than kill Westerners, as was done in Syria, they lined up and executed African Christians, Egyptians, and Ethiopians.

The local IS commander was eventually executed by an al-Qaeda affiliate and they were chased out of Derna, only to set up a new base in Sirte – Gaddafi's tribal home. Benghazi became a daily battleground between Islamist groups and rival militias. Civil war was back. But because of the war in Syria it received very little publicity.

At the beginning of the uprising back in February 2011, Colonel Gaddafi warned that al-Qaeda and other Islamist extremists would take advantage of the instability in his country and Libya would be dismembered. Rather prophetic, don't you think? He knew what would happen in the same way Saddam Hussein knew what would happen if he was taken out of Iraq. Was life better after their regimes were overthrown? It's a question only the people living in those countries can answer.

Chapter 3

DOWNFALL

REVOLUTION IN EGYPT

A red tide swept into Cairo. A flood of fire and rage consumed the great Egyptian capital, engulfing its historic architecture and ancient wonders of the world. What was once a fortress of the Middle East was now a castle built on shifting sands as the people rose up against the power and self-interest of brutal dictator Hosni Mubarak, who had ruled the nation for three decades. Thirty years without change. The people had had enough.

Mubarak rose to power back in 1981 following the assassination of Anwar Sadat. Sadat was a progressive leader and a winner of the Nobel Peace Prize who was gunned down by Muslim extremists during a military parade. Mubarak was Sadat's vice-president and was close by during the attacks but was lucky enough to escape the bullets. His luck would continue over the years as he managed to survive six assassination attempts. Mubarak, like Gaddafi, was a military strongman who ruled by fear and kept the country under emergency law, which meant people lived with heavy restrictions on basic freedoms and anyone could be detained without charge. His government argued that a draconian system was needed to combat Islamic terrorism. But with the passage of time Egypt turned into a police state. Human Rights Watch advocates constantly reported police brutality, persecution of minorities, and suppression of political dissidents. A free media was generally non-existent. Prisons were overcrowded, underfunded, and rampant with abuse and disease. A taxi driver told me about life under the regime where many people lived on just two dollars a day: 'You've got to put up with it. There's nothing you can do about it. There's no choice.' Power breeds greed and corruption and in Africa and the Middle East it's rife, but a downtrodden people can only take so much. After thirty years without succession or change, Egypt's mostly younger generations had had enough of not being able to speak out and they found the courage to rise up against poverty and oppression. The wave of the so-called Arab Spring crashed into town.

From 25 January 2011, government forces and police clashed with protesters across Egypt, from Cairo to Alexandria in the north and to Suez in the east. James and I had been in Qatar covering the final of football's Asian Cup where Australia was playing Japan. We saw the images of utter chaos and bloodshed in Cairo as the revolution got underway. It was a bloody battlefield. A few frustrating flight delays meant we couldn't arrive in the capital until the following afternoon. In Egypt, a state of emergency had been declared and the army had taken over. Night-time curfews were in place. The military patrolled the streets after dark with orders to shoot anyone who disobeyed the curfew.

I was perhaps a little naive at the time. Sometimes that helped. Other times it didn't. James and I arrived without security or even a translator. Remember, the troubles in Egypt came before Libya and Gaza, so we were a little green, a little inexperienced. In the United States I was a member of a larger team but in London it was just me and James, and we were in the process of re-opening the London bureau after it had been closed for years. We hadn't even organised an office before the Arab Spring exploded.

Even though we travelled light, our bags were searched when we landed at Cairo International Airport and most of our equipment was confiscated. James still had one small camera, on which we would have to film everything. Once we finally made it through customs and security, we managed to hitch a ride into town from a local tourist operator who had two middle-aged Australian tourists, Gayle and Terry Hanson, with him. The Hansons were at the start of what they had thought was going to be a dream two-week Egyptian holiday. The driver told us, 'I might not be able to take you all the way to Tahrir Square. There are too many roadblocks and danger. You will have to find other transport to finish the journey.' Money talks. He took us all the way. Like Benghazi during the Libyan crisis, Tahrir Square was the lightning rod of Egypt's revolution. It was in the centre of the city where tens of thousands of anti-government protesters had camped for days in the large concrete square surrounded by shops and shisha cafes. The people carried placards and anti-Mubarak signs. The growing number of occupants drew the ire of heavy-handed police who tried to force the demonstrators out.

•

We had to drive with the curtains in the small van pulled shut because the driver was worried about the military seeing Westerners inside. A few times we came to a stop as we passed military roadblocks and checkpoints. Occasionally, I peeked out as James filmed burning cars and buildings that were ablaze.

We filmed a little sequence with the Hansons. I asked Gayle how concerned she was about the atmosphere in Cairo. She told me, 'All these armoured cars, police and army on the road, I'm frightened out of my wits.'

By the time we arrived at our hotel, it was dark and the curfew was in place. But when we walked outside to capture more scenes for the evening news, we ran into groups of people defying the military orders. They carried steel bars, knives, and machetes to protect themselves from thugs and looters. I'm not sure they knew what to make of us at that point. There were plenty of media around, so we weren't a minority. The crowds looked threatening on camera but didn't attack us. They had more important things to worry about. We finished filming our piece and went back inside.

Both Mubarak supporters and anti-government protesters were out on the streets. At that time, Cairo was one of the most dangerous places in the world because just to walk down the street at night showed a careless disregard for your own life. Most of the Mubarak supporters were the well-off Egyptians; those who worked for the police or the government, or were paid to be there. Life under Mubarak was relatively good for them. The protesters were the ones who had suffered from police brutality, high prices, public censorship and a corrupt government. Over the following days and nights, Tahrir Square became their home. Their neighbours, being fellow occupants, were like-minded people. Same grudges, same grievances.

•

Several days later, James and I were in a taxi, our usual mode of transport in Cairo. Just us and the camera in the back seat of a cab with torn upholstery that burned your skin in the hot sun. We paid the driver the equivalent of a few hundred dollars to drive us away from our hotel and around the capital for a few hours so we could film what was happening in a city under siege.

The driver was a nice enough man who supported the revolution. He told us he had had enough of the corruption and the declining standards of living. The gulf between the rich and poor was far too wide. He said he was too old to join the revolution, but was happy to spectate and leave it to the younger generation to form a new Egypt. That's how many of the older people felt. For too long they had been programmed what to think and what to say – at least publicly. Privately, they may have held different opinions but if they were critical of the government in public it could mean jail or even death. That's what made the revolution so remarkable. People suddenly and openly ignored the demands of the regime and thumbed their collective noses at it.

Our taxi had turned into a back street when it suddenly came to a stop. A man with a creased dark face and who was wearing ordinary clothing and holding a large rusted machete walked up to us and leaned into the taxi. Ominous.

He flashed the machete at the cab driver, then looked at James and me in the back seat. Some Arabic was spoken to the driver. I looked at the blade, and then looked ahead. I didn't want to lock eyes with the man so I tried to act as though shoving a machete in a cab wasn't a thing. The driver continued his conversation in Arabic for a few more moments. It didn't seem to be an aggressive chat. The machete man looked at us again, then pushed himself off the car. Problem solved.

'You need to be careful,' said the driver as he softly pushed the accelerator and carried on down the street. No more words were spoken. I definitely wasn't in Cairns anymore. Journalists were being attacked and beaten by government thugs at this point so I nervously shifted in my hot seat and wondered who that man was – a protester?

A government supporter? An opportunist? He hadn't been that aggressive, but his actions were unnerving. Worse was to come.

A short while after Mr Machete, our taxi was stopped at a roadblock. Some armed men in police uniforms noticed James and me in the back seat and signalled the driver to pull over to the side of the road. Ominous again. This man was much more aggressive. We kept quiet in the back. I tried to look ahead and catch the eye of the driver in his rear-view mirror. He looked up with a sweaty face, saw me looking at him and then quickly looked away. That wasn't good.

The policeman hit my window with his hand and waved for us to get out of the car. The driver said he was sorry but we had to get out. 'You have to go with them now and take your equipment,' he said. We didn't have much equipment anyway as most of it had been confiscated at the airport on arrival. But it was not the time or place to refuse any sort of command, so James and I climbed out of the car, lifted our tripod and sound bag from the boot, and were marched by the police a few hundred metres down the road. Cars were slowly driving past and people were staring at us as we were led to a makeshift police station underneath a dark bridge along the River Nile.

I looked nervously at the dark water beside us, knowing that throughout history a lot of problems had been solved in that dirty river.

The station had been squared off with blue tarps so no one could peer in. We were led inside and found a rectangular desk, sitting at which was someone who appeared to be a higher-ranking police officer. There were lots of badges on his chest and shoulder. We were here for a grilling. A few other officers stood behind us as we were questioned. Being Australian helped because at that point the Egyptian government didn't have any beef with us, but I was still very nervous. We had to hand over our passports. As the main officer flicked through them, I thanked my lucky stars that I wasn't carrying my other passport – it was in my bag back at the hotel. I always travelled with two: one that allowed access to Israel; another for Arab countries. Most journalists had two for that reason. Never mix and never get the two confused. If an Israeli stamp was seen in an Arab country, you could be labelled an Israeli spy. That could mean a beating, or worse.

'What are you doing here?' was the first question.

'We are here to cover the revolution,' I replied.

'What revolution? There is no revolution,' came the terse response. The officer continued, 'That, out there, is just drunk behaviour. Who do you work for?'

'Channel Nine Australia.'

He gave a quizzical look to one of his lieutenants who shrugged his shoulder.

'Are you American? CNN? BBC? Al-Jazeera?' the interrogation continued.

'No,' I said. 'We are Australian. You know . . . kangaroo.' I mimicked a roo jump.

The mood shifted slightly as a hint of a smile came across my interrogator's face. He turned to a page of my passport that had a Qatar stamp. 'What is this?' he asked. Egypt had a problem with the al-Jazeera news network, which was based in Qatar and had links to the West. It was possibly a troubling development for us.

'Football,' I told the officer and mimed kicking an imaginary ball. 'Australia was in the final of the Asian Cup against Japan so we were in Doha reporting on the game, but then we were sent here instead.' The mood lifted slightly again at the mention of the world game, football. I sensed that we would be okay. The officer took a deep breath, leaned back in his chair and gave us a good stare. Then, after a few more tense moments of silence, he tossed the passports on the plastic table and waved us away. Kangaroos and football saved us. I felt a great sense of relief.

The officer who had originally detained us shoved us out of the makeshift station and told us to get back to our hotel. In the hot sun, we walked the few hundred metres to the Ramses Hilton, where most media were staying. We'd had a close call but much more was to come.

•

It was Thursday, 2 February 2011. Midday in Cairo. The hot, humid air was punctured by a bright sun that beat down on a capital simmering with tension. Prayers were underway. It was as if the masses were cleansing their souls to make room for sin. Hundreds of men formed long straight lines, dozens of rows deep, as they stood with their eyes closed, palms opened skywards, while a chorus of gentle voices whispered messages to their almighty. The men were dressed in casual clothing, some with footwear, some without. They lowered themselves to the ground and folded their bodies over a mat or small rug to allow their foreheads to kiss the earth. I observed from the side and wondered what it would be like to believe so strongly. To know with absolute certainty what world exists beyond our own; where we go after we die. I wondered the same thing at the Papal Conclave years later as thousands of Catholic pilgrims descended on Rome.

The men and boys I was watching were the ones who had been camped in Tahrir Square for days in the hope that their opposition to President Hosni Mubarak would oust him from office. They were some of Egypt's best and brightest, including students, academics, athletes, and doctors. At that point they didn't know, although they might have guessed, that in other parts of the city men aligned with the pugnacious president were saying prayers of their own, kneeling to the same god and asking for forgiveness before God had any reason to forgive.

During the Arab Spring, these 'days of rage' were usually accompanied by a big bloody fight. What we didn't bank on was how violent the day would become as the anti- and pro-Mubarak forces clashed after lunchtime prayers.

The public prayers only lasted for a few minutes and then the chants began. 'The people want the fall of the regime,' they shouted. The large crowd of mostly men and teenage boys assembled in their concrete battleground, which was Tahrir Square or Independence Square – the great tabernacle of the resistance. They waved anti-regime banners and demanded Mubarak give up or leave office. But dictators don't just give up. Not yet, anyway.

James and I were filming around the edges of the square where thousands of people cried for their freedom. 'Mubarak must go,' they told me. 'He must go now!' It was all done for the cameras so the rest of the world could see. While the media weren't the ones demanding Mubarak's removal, we were in effect the mouthpieces of the revolution because we broadcast their messages far beyond Egyptian borders.

The government had switched off internet access, which made it difficult to get messages out. But some groups were able to rally crowds through social media platforms such as Twitter and Facebook. They called it the Facebook revolution.

As we stood watching the people chanting in the square, it all seemed fairly calm and positive, but then the dark clouds rolled in with sudden destructive winds.

James and I saw incoming pro-Mubarak supporters walking up the street towards us, so we approached them to ask a few questions. They roasted me with a fire-breathing rage. A group of them surrounded our camera and yelled full support for their beleaguered president. The men were so close I could see the veins in their necks pop out and the blood rise to their faces. They'd obviously had enough of

Tahrir's occupation and they were going to do something about it.

After the pro-Mubarak demonstrators had their say with us, James and I looked at each other and immediately set out for the square knowing full well that some heavy shit was about to go down. The time had come for the sides to face off. We positioned ourselves in the centre of the square, which was about the size of a football field. We were effectively at the halfway line between the two sets of supporters. There, we surmised, we would get the initial shots of them crashing against each other like those armies in old war movies, but without the weapons. This is it, we thought. Prime position.

Occasionally a low-flying military jet would roar above us in the hope that the deafening noise would disperse the crowds. No chance. The two sides shouted their respective chants at each other before they collided like two strong opposing currents of water. What James and I didn't factor in was their size. The numbers of anti- and pro-Mubarak protesters were so big that we were pushed off to the side of the square and our bodies were squashed against a small sharp side gate. Had we stayed in that position we could have been crushed by the sheer volume of people, so we climbed over the gate. As the tension rose, a sense of nervous exhilaration came over me. Something big was about to happen and we were here for it.

The two sides now occupied the huge square. We couldn't really film much at ground level. We needed to get higher. We saw a garbage truck parked close by so we climbed up the back of it and dropped into the tray, which was full of rubbish. Every step we took our legs sank into a thick soup of muck and filth. It was hard not to laugh at the absurdity of our situation as the two sets of protesters hurled abuse at each other a few feet below us. We filmed for a short while as things dangerously escalated with every passing second.

After a while, the garbage truck became too unstable so we jumped off and landed back in the mire of protesters. They pushed and shoved each other, but the crowds wouldn't disperse or separate. Then a few gaps appeared. Confused and scared, people dashed back and forth as pockets of space opened up between the two warring sides. I wondered what on earth had caused it, until I was struck. A sharp rock hit me on the shoulder, then another hit me on the leg. It felt like I had been pinged by sharp and heavy hailstones. James and I ducked for cover and raced to the side of the square while hundreds of sharp objects – rocks and small, broken pieces of concrete – flew through the air. I'd never seen anything like it before.

The riot had become a rock fight. Protesters were smashing the concrete ground so that it churned up little pieces that could then be used as projectiles. People with bruised and bloodied faces rushed past us.

James and I were sucked into the back streets, where the larger fight on Tahrir splintered into smaller rock fights. We later found out that this was where other journalists got into trouble. The BBC's Jeremy Bowen was accosted.

CNN's Anderson Cooper was roughed up and had to flee. Big TV names were attacked. James and I were right in it but Jimmy had dreadlocks so he didn't look like a typical cameraman. I think the Egyptians liked the look of him. The ones we were with, anyway.

It was hard to know exactly which side we were with as fighters cracked the concrete ground and hurled heavy pieces at the opposing side. It was about then that one of the defining images of the Egyptian revolution took place, as a dozen or so Mubarak supporters charged into the crowd on camels, carrying pictures of their president. It was very strange, but these were strange times.

The camel riders whipped protesters with sticks until one of them was yanked off the animal and was set upon by a group of protesters and beaten on the ground. Eventually, the riders were outnumbered and were all chased away.

We were told to stop filming. 'It's not safe for you here,' one of the fighters told us, so we backtracked through the streets and returned to Tahrir Square where another group of men surrounded us. They grappled and grabbed at James's backpack and demanded to know who we were. The fighter who'd originally told us to leave had come with us – perhaps he suspected we might be in for a spot of bother – and told the others to calm down. We carried on back to our hotel, which overlooked the square and was only about a hundred metres away.

On the way back to the safety of the hotel, I saw a man with long bread rolls – the kind you use for hot dogs – taped to his head. It was funny at first but then I realised the rolls were padding to protect his head against the rock missiles. So many of the rock fighters suffered serious head wounds and had gashes across their faces following direct hits from the sharp concrete weaponry.

During all of this fighting at Tahrir Square, the police and the military were nowhere to be seen. Perhaps because they had other people do their dirty work. Some of the pro-Mubarak supporters were on the government payroll so the order was to get rid of the demonstrators, no matter the cost. Despite curfews, the fighting continued well into the night. The weapons became more deadly and I could hear the occasional crackle of gunfire as armoured tanks rolled in. The darkness of the night was lit up by the burning frontlines. A Molotov cocktail was thrown from end to end of the square, leaving behind a fire trail. Wounded fighters recovered inside buildings and mosques within the square.

It was like this for many more nights and many more days. The population of protesters swelled, and signs written in English were painted for the Western media to film. Barricades became taller and security checks leading into the square were tighter. The protesters had bunkered down and were ready for more.

•

During the beginning of the unrest James and I stayed at the Ramses Hilton in Cairo, which was the hotel where most of the foreign press stayed. But as the protests continued, the

Mubarak regime started to blame Western media outlets for fuelling the unrest. Gaddafi was to do the same. The regime held a particularly strong disregard for American and British journalists and those from the English version of the al-Jazeera network.

But there were so many foreign journalists in Egypt by then that Mubarak's security forces couldn't silence the entire pack. Instead, they tried to threaten and intimidate us. Some reporters who broadcast live from balconies overlooking Tahrir Square had their lights shot at. Local news facilities that we were using to cross live into the *Today* show and Channel Nine national evening news bulletins had their broadcast cables cut. The secret police were cutting broadcasting cables so no one could report live. Signals were going dead across the city. The regime was trying to create an information vacuum and, out on the streets, violent chaos reigned. It's still the most intimidating environment I've ever reported from.

One evening during the height of the crisis, when strict curfews were in place, James had to wait until the middle of the night to walk out onto the streets to set up his portable satellite dish, called a BGAN, which allowed him to send our footage and our story back to Sydney. It makes a faint beeping noise as it searches for satellites to lock onto. When the military patrolled the streets close by he had to dive behind bushes to hide himself. He didn't get much sleep that night.

The next day it became clear that we had to move hotels. Reporters were getting kidnapped, beaten and tortured. A friend of mine, Greg Palkot, a correspondent from America's Fox network, was hit by a Molotov cocktail and severely beaten by a group of pro-Mubarak thugs after someone accused him of being an Israeli spy.

Things came to a head when I walked across the busy lobby and saw the concierge passing handguns to staff. They were keeping weapons and ammunition behind the desk as a precaution. 'What's going on?' I asked. 'Don't worry, you will be safe,' I was told. It didn't fill me with a great deal of confidence, especially when I saw other hotel workers boarding up the glass windows and doors that led out to the street.

James and I shifted a few streets back, to the more secure Fairmont Hotel where Australian tourists were being kept by consular officials. I remember the day we moved because it was the only time I got a phone call from Channel Nine's CEO at the time, David Gyngell.

'You all right, mate?' he asked.

'Yeah, we're fine.'

'Good, because I don't have any life insurance for you!' he joked.

We had a laugh and carried on.

Dozens of Australians were trapped in Cairo during the uprising and were desperate to get home. Cairo International Airport had become a cluttered hostel after thousands of tourists camped there, hoping for seats on emergency flights out. Long queues of people filled the departure areas and snaked outside the building. Some Australians I spoke to had slept on the airport's concrete floors for four straight nights. One of them described the desperate conditions to me: 'We really don't want to go back to the hotel but we can't stay here for long. There are no banks open so there's no money and there's no food left. It's absolutely chaotic.'

Qantas and our government came to the rescue as extra flights were put on to help clear the backlog of stranded Australians.

•

On the night of 11 February, as I was tucking into a delicious plate of Koshari, the national dish of Egypt, it all came to an end. The pressure valve burst open. 'Hosni Mubarak has resigned,' Vice-President Omar Suleiman announced, and Tahrir Square erupted in celebration. After thirty years holding onto power, Mubarak lost it in just eighteen days.

We in the West can sometimes take freedoms for granted, but on that historic evening I learned what it is like to finally have freedom after it has long been denied. James and I rushed to the square along with hundreds of people who wanted to join their brothers in victory. Young Egyptians, the hope for the future, sat on the shoulders of family and friends and raised their arms into the air. Tahrir Square was crammed with up to 100,000 people who celebrated as if their nation had won a world cup or a huge sporting competition. 'Mubarak took everything from us. We have been afraid for thirty years. No one is afraid now,' I was told. The people held their anti-regime banners and waved Egyptian flags, but most importantly, they smiled. It had been a while since they had experienced this kind of freedom. 'This is the spirit of the Egyptian people. We have been born again!' One after another, they spoke about the weight of dictatorship that had been lifted from their oppressed shoulders. 'Egypt is newborn! Egypt has freedom!'

Freedom had come at a cost though. Throughout the course of the revolution up to 1000 people were killed or went missing, while another 6000 were injured.

Soon enough, the tributes came in from foreign governments.

When the revolution had begun, US President Barack Obama had sided with the protesters and, as is usually the case, most of the West had followed suit. Australia, Britain, and France had fallen into line behind America and called for democratic reform without really suggesting who should be the successor. That was Egypt's job.

When Mubarak was overthrown, Obama led the championing of people power: 'There are very few moments in our lives where we have the privilege to witness history taking place.'

Australian Prime Minister Kevin Rudd paid tribute to the protesters who were collectively named as *Time* magazine's 2011 person of the year: 'We've seen the people of Egypt speak loudly, clearly, courageously, peacefully, and effectively.'

UK Prime Minister David Cameron spoke of his hope for the future: 'Those who now run Egypt have a duty to reflect the issues of Egyptian people.'

It was a rare night in Egypt when women felt safe enough to be outdoors. Hundreds of traditionally dressed women celebrated into the night with their male friends and families. There didn't seem to be any reason to be afraid. Ironically, it was on this night when an awfully violent attack occurred on a female journalist. Well-known CBS reporter Lara Logan was viciously beaten and sexually assaulted by a mob of at least two hundred men. As the city celebrated its supposed freedom, a Western woman was taken from the crowd and raped by a pack of wild animals. It tarnished the country's greatest night in many long years. Perhaps it was also a sign that the country wasn't ready to be free. Oppression wasn't completely dead, and soon it would roar back to life.

•

After Mubarak's resignation, Egypt lived in a state of fragile peace. Following the 2011 uprising, Mohamed Morsi became the nation's first ever democratically elected president. Egypt was the great hope of the Middle East and many people were watching to see how a dictatorship could be successfully transformed into a democracy. It didn't last long.

Morsi was a leading member of the Sunni Islamist Muslim Brotherhood organisation, and his rule was shambolic. The economy tanked because tourism crashed, violence soared and there were increased sexual assaults against women on the street. Morsi imposed strict Islamist views across the government and the state, and he wasn't inclusive to other bureaucrats when he said he would be, so demonstrations broke out. Small ones at first, which led to much larger rallies. Things got worse. In July 2013, the head of the army – General Abdel Fattah el-Sisi – gave Morsi forty-eight hours to step aside. When he didn't, troops stormed in and removed him. He had been president for barely a year.

Morsi's supporters were deeply unhappy about his removal. Thousands of Muslim Brotherhood members and supporters set up two large protest camps in Cairo, similar to the sit-in at Tahrir Square two years earlier. It was a focal point for stoushes and clashes between rival groups of supporters – those who were for Morsi and those who were against. The military was in charge and thought the camps were destabilising the nation and preventing it from moving towards a new election so, after six weeks, orders were given for the tens of thousands of protesters to move on. The protesters wouldn't budge. In August the order came for security forces to systematically and methodically clear the protest camps out by any means necessary. Squads of police, snipers, tanks, and helicopters moved in for a swift armoured assault and turned the camps into killing fields. It was barbaric and ruthless. Men and women, boys and girls were trapped and murdered in cold blood. Bodies and buildings were burned during a massacre that lasted up to twelve hours.

I watched in shock and horror from London as pictures of the attack came in. Human rights advocates reported that security forces had fired guns into makeshift hospitals to finish many victims off. The known death toll topped 1000 in what Amnesty International called Egypt's darkest day, and Human Rights Watch described as 'the largest mass killing of protesters in a single day in recent history'.

I called my boss, Darren Wick, and said I needed to go to Egypt to cover events. Usually Wickie never hesitated to green-light a mission, but he had reservations about this one because journalists were being attacked and killed. Veteran British cameraman Mick Deane, who James and I had met in Libya, had been shot and killed by a sniper a few days earlier. I convinced Wickie that the story needed to be covered and it was approved on the proviso that I take much more care than usual. Deal.

I took the night flight and arrived in Cairo the following day with cameraman Dan Guia. It was extremely unsettling because the media on the ground were all nervous after Mick's death. It could happen to any of us if we weren't careful. Dan and I went straight to Rabaa Square, the scene of the massacre. I stood in the blackened shell of a building where many people had been mercilessly gunned down. The bodies had been moved to morgues but the square was still a mess and the smell was a pungent mix of putrid death and burnt rubber. There were bullet holes in walls and dried blood on the ground. Bulldozers came in to clear up the rubbish. Dozens of police officers stood in the square and kept a close eye on us as we filmed. It's hard to believe but I felt less safe than I did in 2011 – and that was the most intimidated I had ever been.

It was killing season in Egypt and it wasn't over yet. Retribution was planned the following day.

Over the years reporting from the Middle East, I came to find the sounds of the Muslim call to prayer somewhat comforting. I liked listening to it. Sometimes it would puncture the silence of a day as I stared out across whatever city I was in. But other times it filled me with dread and anxiety. That was the case on 16 August 2013. Morsi's supporters wanted him reinstated and so they called for a 'day of rage' after Friday prayers. I knew exactly what was coming. There was an eerie sense of deja vu about it. The prayers, the folded bodies on mats, the heat, the tension, and then it began. The rage. It started off with a chant. Then it got louder and louder as more people joined in. Muslim Brotherhood supporters had called on their followers to march on Ramses Square after they'd finished at the mosques of Cairo. So, very quickly, after midday, the square became cramped and crowded. Dan and I were getting squeezed out and pushed around as thousands of angry sweaty bodies demanded justice for their toppled leader.

Western leaders were very careful not to call Morsi's removal a coup. But it was. A coup is a coup, just like war is war. Military helicopters occasionally flew overhead as the large crowd shouted in full voice. They were ready for an assault. I asked a man who stood nearby with his son if he was happy to die that day. He looked at me and said, 'If that's what it takes then, yes, I will die.' It was almost as if the Arab Spring hadn't even existed.

I saw snipers gathering on the rooftops. They stood and watched at first. Some were grouped in twos and threes while others stood on their own. That was as sure a sign as any that my time there was done. I wasn't going to get caught when the bullets rained down. Dan and I slowly squeezed through the growing crowd and made our way out of the square. A few moments later, canisters of tear gas were dropped in. Then it was on.

Bullets rained down from the snipers on the rooftops and from plain-clothed officers on nearby bridges. While I was in the square, I didn't see a single protester who was armed. Civilians were caught in the crossfire. Mosques quickly became hospitals and a thick grey smoke filled the square.

I had left the death zone just in time and relied heavily for information and footage from our affiliate media crews, such as the Reuters news agency, and citizen cameramen who posted their images online.

In the central al-Fateh mosque, bodies covered the bloodstained carpet as more dead and wounded victims were carried in. Ten, twenty, forty dead. It didn't stop there. As thick pools of blood drenched the clothing of wounded victims, the tally of incoming corpses rose even higher. Forty, eighty, it kept on going. Doctors tried desperately to save lives but they were helpless in the face of such brutality. The firing stopped at dusk and the bodies were transported to hospitals.

Ordinary citizens were gunned down for nothing. The simple act of a peaceful protest could cost you your life. I wondered about the man I had spoken to earlier. Had he and his son survived?

The next day, Dan and I were filming outside the al-Fateh mosque where dozens of protesters had barricaded themselves in overnight. As we filmed, armoured tanks arrived. I saw a young man bolt from the side door of the mosque. He looked like a teenager. A small group of policemen chased after him, until one of them stopped, raised his rifle, looked through the barrel, and fired his weapon. The young man fell to the ground. It happened in the space of about fifteen seconds. Next the police stormed the mosque, throwing tear gas and firing their weapons at those left inside. They were even shooting at the sacred minarets. A short while later the final protesters were dragged out. The protest was over. They would be taken to jail where they would most likely be tortured or beaten.

An interim government was installed and less than a year later, in June 2014, Abdel Fattah el-Sisi was voted in as the next president. A military man was back in the seat of power. In the short space of three years, Egypt had turned full circle from Mubarak, to Morsi, to el-Sisi. El-Sisi's government stressed a need to be tough because of the constant threat of Islamic militants. The new president took notes from the Mubarak playbook and cracked down on political dissent and protests. Activists and journalists were beaten and locked up, while plain-clothed officers roamed the streets. There were continuing reports of abuse against citizens, but it seemed as though the West was once again happy to ignore what was going on. Maybe it was just easier that way.

Welcome to the new Egypt. It's much like the old one.

Chapter 4

JE SUIS PARIS

TERROR IN EUROPE

Central Paris, 7 January 2015. Just before lunchtime. A storm was coming.

On a cold and cloudy day, two hooded gunmen dressed in black clothing got out of a small black Citroën C3. They carried Kalashnikov assault rifles and purposefully strode up to the building that housed the weekly French satirical magazine called *Charlie Hebdo*. For many years the magazine had made fun of the Prophet Muhammad, as well as Islam, just as it also targeted Christianity and Judaism. Everyone and everything was fair game. Satire had become dangerous though and *Charlie Hebdo* had had to install security at its front doors and provide bodyguards for the magazine's editors.

In the city's busy 11th district the men burst into number 6 Rue Nicolas-Appert and shouted, 'Is this *Charlie Hebdo*?'

No, it wasn't. They had the wrong address. The target was down the street. Number 10. The city was about to suffer its biggest terror attack in more than forty years and the nation would be held hostage for several days.

The terrorists, who would later be known around the world as brothers Said and Cherif Kouachi, approached the building. They needed a code that would grant them access past the security doors. They didn't have it but they found someone who did. Cartoonist Corinne Rey, who publishes under her pen-name Coco, had just returned to work after having picked up her daughter from day care. Talk about wrong place, wrong time. The young mother was given a terrifying and dreadful ultimatum by the men who apparently spoke perfect French and claimed to be from al-Qaeda. Enter the code or be killed. Rey reluctantly gave them the code, not knowing if she was going to survive. The brothers then calmly walked through the doors and immediately sprayed the lobby with gunfire.

Their first victim was a maintenance worker who had been sitting at reception. Rey was not out of trouble yet. Held at gunpoint, she was forced to lead the men up to the *Charlie Hebdo* newsroom on the second floor where the cartoonists and journalists were holding their first editorial meeting of the year. Up to fifteen staff members, who were all seated around a large oval table, heard the gunshots from the floor below but mistakenly assumed they were firecrackers and carried on with what was described as a lively editorial debate. In an interview with France's *Le*

Parisien newspaper, *Charlie Hebdo*'s investigative reporter Laurent Leger said everyone had just returned to work after the Christmas holidays so they were happy and in good form, almost celebrating the new year ahead. Then the doors to the meeting room were thrust open.

'We still thought it was a joke. The atmosphere was still joyous. But then we smelled the strong odour of gunpowder in the corridor, and we all realised that this wasn't a joke at all,' Leger told the newspaper.

Leger, who was sitting with his back to the door, said that's when the gunmen opened fire and he dived for cover. One by one, the brothers called out names and executed many of the *Charlie Hebdo* staff. It was clear they had come in with a plan and it was brutally delivered. An editor and his bodyguard, cartoonists and journalists, were shot in the head during a killing spree that lasted between five and ten minutes. A flash of time that left a horrendous mark of blood and death on the office floor. Eleven people were killed and eleven others were injured.

Corinne Rey was still alive, and now hiding under a desk. She saw the men line up a female colleague but decide against killing her. Ms Rey told police she heard one of the men tell her friend, 'I'm not killing you because you are a woman and we don't kill women. But you have to convert to Islam, read the Quran, and wear a veil.'

It wasn't true. They had already gunned down another female journalist.

The men then left shouting *'Allahu Akbar'*. But the massacre wasn't over.

Police had been alerted to an attack and they arrived at the scene as the killers were making their escape. As the men scurried away from the building and into a waiting getaway car, driven by a third man, online video showed a police vehicle had blocked their exit route. Very calmly, the brothers got out of the black hatchback, fired shots at the police car, and smashed its windows. The Kouachis clearly knew how to handle guns and it was suggested at the time that they might have had some form of military training.

Further up the street, they found wounded police officer Ahmed Merabet lying on the footpath. Forty-year-old Merabet had been patrolling the 11th district on his bike. It was his last day of bicycle duty before a promotion. According to reports, Merabet had fired his police-issued pistol at the terrorists as they fled the *Charlie Hebdo* building but it was no match for the return fire of the AK-47 and he was struck. Merabet lay wounded on the footpath. One of the brothers approached with his automatic weapon raised and reportedly asked him, 'You want to kill us?' The injured officer replied, 'No, it's fine, boss' and raised his arm over his head, perhaps expecting a bullet would come. It did. Merabet was shot in the head and the death toll was now at twelve.

The Kouachis then returned to their getaway car, job done, and shouted, 'We have avenged the Prophet Muhammad. We have killed *Charlie Hebdo*!' and then disappeared into the city. Both the Kouachis and their driver had their faces covered so they couldn't be identified. It seemed they thought they would get away alive.

Merabet's cold-blooded shooting proved the attack was not just about silencing the critics of the Prophet Muhammad. Merabet was Muslim – the same religion as both of the Kouachi brothers. As the French President François Hollande said at the police officer's funeral, 'Ahmed Merabet knew better than anyone that radical Islam has nothing to do with Islam and that fanaticism kills Muslims.' The president went on to claim that Merabet was a symbol of the diversity of France's law and order. Unfortunately for Merabet, he was just in the wrong place.

Most of the time, a terror attack is over before it even makes the news and attracts world attention. This was certainly true in the first part of this case. Shortly after the brothers had cruelly ended a dozen lives, traumatised a dozen more and then disappeared into the Parisian suburbs, news reports began to emerge of a terror attack in the French capital. It's the kind of stuff that grabs your attention quickly. I was in London and had Sky News on the television and, when the anchor threw to live pictures of a smashed police car and armed officers outside a building, I made immediate plans to move. I rushed to the Eurostar and caught the next train across the English Channel. Cameraman Andrew Greaves, producer Eliza Berkery and reporter Andrew Lund joined me.

About four hours later, I was outside the *Charlie Hebdo* office as I prepared to report live on the *Today* show to recap the heartbreaking events of the afternoon. A grim, unsettling silence had fallen over the beautiful city. Parisians were stunned. They lit candles and left flowers outside the magazine's front door, on the streets and in the gardens nearby. As night fell, word quickly spread of a rally down the street. At a grand monument in a city square called Place de la République, thousands of people gathered in solidarity. They held signs that read 'Not Afraid' – a message to anyone who threatened France's '*Liberté, Égalité, Fraternité*' (Liberty, Equality, Fraternity), a motto founded during the French Revolution. The signs were mostly symbolic because people were afraid. But, in true French style, they were flipping the bird to the antagonists. Another motto was born that evening. One that quickly spread throughout the world and became a symbol of the terror strike: *Je suis Charlie* – I am Charlie. We all were.

The attack wasn't just a murderous rampage that resulted in the loss of innocent civilians, it was an attempt to silence freedom of speech and a free media. That's a right people have bled and died for. It's not a right everyone has. As a Western journalist I am fully aware how lucky we are to have it and, consequently, have never taken it for granted. This was not just an assault on peace-loving people but an assault on my profession. Comedians around the world also expressed shock and dismay because it was also an attempt to silence humour. One of the great tributes that I saw was people leaving pens and pencils with the flowers and candles. They were encouraging the ink to continue to flow. For people to continue writing words. To continue telling jokes. To continue telling stories. To borrow an old cliché, the pen is indeed mightier than the sword. I felt like everyone appreciated that a little more.

On the next day, a minute's silence was observed around the country. At midday, the bells at the Notre Dame cathedral sounded to mark the start of the occasion. I happened to be at the Place de la République where hundreds of people formed a giant circle around the monument, which was full of tributes for the victims. People held hands and linked arms in an incredibly emotional moment. It was pouring down with rain but it didn't stop the mourners as Paris fell silent. Then, at its completion, everyone broke out into spontaneous applause. Friends held friends. Strangers hugged strangers. Well done, Paris. A classy touch.

But no one could quite relax. There was a tense undercurrent. The city had just lost part of its soul and people were still frightened. And there was a very good reason why. The killers were still on the loose.

•

It was 9 January 2015, two days after the attack, and Paris was still on edge. The city was being held hostage. Armed police patrolled famous landmarks including the Eiffel Tower, the Arc de Triomphe, along the Champs-Élysées, the Louvre, and anywhere tourists gathered. Sirens blared with unnerving regularity and I was as sick as a dog. A man-flu had brought me down, which frustrated me to no end when there was a major international story to cover. French authorities were now involved in one of the largest manhunts in the country's history. Despite the Kouachi brothers' attempts to conceal their faces, the police had quickly identified them as the main suspects for the *Charlie Hebdo* attack. The brothers, 34-year-old Said Kouachi and 32-year-old Cherif Kouachi, were on the run.

People had started to piece together some of the brothers' story. Born in Paris to Algerian immigrants, they both held a mighty grudge. Their life had been tough from the start and the path to terror began early. According to French news website *Reporterre*, they grew up in the poor suburbs of Paris and their father died when they were young. They were left to roam around housing estates while their mother turned to prostitution to pay the bills. When the brothers were in their early teens she died from an apparent drug overdose, which may have been deliberate. The brothers were brought up in a children's home. According to reports, they smoked pot and drank alcohol while earning a small income from low-paying jobs. They eventually became members of a gang that included other disenfranchised youths and Muslim leaders with extreme views, and so were lured into the world of jihad.

In about 2004, when the Iraq War was in full swing, Cherif Kouachi was appalled at what he felt were injustices committed by American troops, so he turned himself to the jihad cause. But before he could travel to Iraq, he was picked up by police and arrested. That's when the real radicalisation set in. Kouachi was in prison with other hardliners and recruiters of the European networks of al-Qaeda. He met another disaffected youth named Amedy Coulibaly, who would join the Kouachi brothers in plotting the 2015 assault on Paris.

Two days after they had gunned down twelve people in the French capital, the Kouachi brothers' trail was picked up by police. There had been near misses and close calls but nothing to bring the manhunt to an end. Then came a sighting at a petrol station a few dozen kilometres outside Paris. The brothers had hijacked another small car. The police chase ramped up, and we joined the action.

Andrew and I didn't have a car so we hired a taxi for the day. Reports were coming through of a police chase along the highway close to Charles de Gaulle Airport where twin runways were closed to allow police helicopters into the sky. Following the breadcrumbs of information that were leaked on social media sites such as Twitter, we were able to track the police movements and easily report on the chase. It was about ten o'clock in the morning, which was about 8 pm Australian Eastern time, so we didn't have a news bulletin to feature on but I chipped in with a few crosses to Australian radio stations.

Eventually we made it to a place called Dammartin, about ten kilometres away from the airport. The sky was grey and the winds were cold as rain fell, making visibility quite low.

By the time we got to Dammartin, dozens of news crews were already in place. Police had cordoned off a signage production company inside an industrial estate where the brothers had holed up. French police don't muck around, and so the number of armed officers who had descended on the township was significant. More than forty-eight hours of terror were about to come to a dramatic close. The brothers were trapped inside the building and there was no way they were going to escape. It was a full-blown siege and it was going to end in their arrest or death.

We tried to get as close as possible to the scene but we were kept too far back to see much. All we could do was wait while residents and school students in the area were evacuated by bus. Sieges take time. They can last for hours, even days. Police don't know what traps might be indoors, and those who are inside are usually too scared to face what's outside. So it becomes a tense standoff while negotiators try to do their bit.

All we could do was stand and wait in the cold and listen for gunshots that occasionally crackled.

Then the day took another twist. There were reports of another potential terror attack back in Paris. A man and a woman had apparently taken hostages at a Jewish kosher supermarket in Porte de Vincennes to the east of the capital. This is where Amedy Coulibaly, the friend of the Kouachis who was also radicalised in prison, comes in. He was a Parisian born to immigrant parents from Mali, and he had pledged allegiance to the Islamic State. He had already gunned down an unarmed female police officer on the street the day before.

Since we couldn't see much in Dammartin, and we couldn't possibly know how long the siege would last, I decided to dash to the hostage crisis in the capital's 20th district. It was a slow and frustrating drive as traffic had built up around Porte de Vincennes when police shut much of it down. I finally arrived to find queues of armed policemen unloading from large vans and marching to the scene. They were dressed in flak jackets and carried assault rifles. It was pretty clear Coulibaly was about to be taken out. A few hours earlier, he'd walked into the supermarket and sprayed it with gunfire. Armed with a submachine gun, an assault rifle and two pistols, he'd killed four Jewish shoppers within seconds. Coulibaly kept the remaining customers as hostages. He was interviewed by French news network BFMTV during the crisis and he told his interviewer that his motive was revenge. He said he targeted Jews to defend Muslims, Palestinians in particular. His attack was retaliation for Western government actions in Mali, Iraq and Syria.

Hours passed. Coulibaly and the Kouachis were reportedly staying in touch with each other through their mobile phones as their respective sieges progressed.

Whether it was planned or not, both sieges ended at almost the same time in a dramatic and bloody finale. At Dammartin, police slowly crept up on the building where the Kouachi brothers were hiding with two hostages. The brothers must have seen something, or suspected the end was close, so they decided they would die on their terms, as martyrs. They charged out of the building with their guns blazing, Hollywood-style. Within seconds, they were dead.

A few minutes later, police seized their chance at the kosher supermarket, where up to fifteen people were still being kept as hostages. The police traded gunfire with Coulibaly as flash grenades were thrown in to disorient him and explosion after explosion sounded from the store. Coulibaly was dead within seconds and hostages bolted out of the store, including a woman with her young child. Footage from that moment shows the terror and fear on the faces of the hostages. Afterwards, police found explosives tied to a detonator. Five people were killed in the kosher supermarket attack, including the gunman Amedy Coulibaly. But Coulibaly's wife, Hayat Boumeddiene, who had helped him plan the attack, had fled the country days beforehand. She was believed to be in Syria, the heartland of the Islamic State. At the time of writing, she is still France's most wanted woman.

The deaths of the Kouachi brothers and Amedy Coulibaly brought an end to three days of terror in the French capital. Sixteen innocent lives were brutally taken by three terrorists. The attacks were the worst within France's borders in more than forty years. But this terrible reign was over and Parisians could now breathe again. The first step in the healing process was to mourn the dead and show the world they were okay.

•

The numbers defied belief. A million people were expected to march for the victims of France's terror attacks. In the end, on 11 January 2015, four days after the attacks, more than 3.5 million people marched across the nation. An estimated 1.6 million people stood together in Paris alone, which the government later said was a record. It was defiance at its most magnificent, or *magnifique* if you prefer.

I hoped to walk with them, but there were too many people crammed into the city streets so we all just kind of stood together. I was still fairly crook, but the walk was too important to miss. I remember standing with my producer Eliza, who is significantly shorter than I am, and all I could see was the colour white and I started to sway. I was sure I was about to hit the deck. I needed to find some space because I was overheating. So in that beautiful moment of solidarity, in the middle of winter, as a city had come together, an Australian was ripping his jacket and jumpers off and stripping down to a sweaty T-shirt. I had this slightly amusing fear that Eliza was going to have to drag me out of there through the vast field of people. Fortunately, I came around.

The people marching that day included world leaders, the families of victims, and the survivors. People carried flags, and signs that read *'Je suis Charlie'*. They sang the French national anthem together, and vowed not to be defeated. They insisted that terrorism and extremism would not win.

France has the highest percentage Muslim population in Europe and, while most of the country's Muslims are peaceful and patriotic, a select few have given the faith a rotten name. In the outer suburbs of Paris, where salaries are as low as expectations, violence begets violence and extremist elements appear to be flourishing. Tragically, this problem would be exposed again in November 2015 with the attacks at Stade de France, the Bataclan theatre and Parisian restaurants and cafes, which killed 130 people.

The Paris terror attacks of January and November 2015 were designed to fracture French society and stir religious tensions. The government of France, along with other nations, has a huge task ahead of them to make sure the extremists don't succeed. But if the march of the millions was anything to go by, the end result wasn't fractious but unifying.

•

There were times on the road when big news would break and I had to drop everything and get to the story as quickly as possible. Sometimes there was a double-up – when one big story broke at the same time as another. When that happened, I had to decide which story was the better or more powerful one to report on, and then travel to it. Once in my career, three big stories broke at the same time.

On 22 July 2011, I was in Grenoble in eastern France preparing to cover the second-last stage of the Tour de France. Australian Cadel Evans was the frontrunner and had stretched his lead to a point where he couldn't realistically be overtaken. In two days, Cadel Evans would cycle up the famed Champs-Élysées and become the first Australian to win the gruelling race. We were there, ready to report on the climax of the great race and capture his monumental achievement.

As we prepared our report that evening for the *Today* show, news broke from Oslo. A man had gone on a wild shooting rampage and gunned down dozens of people in cold blood. We decided that we would have to leave the Tour and head to Oslo where the death toll was still climbing. When we arrived in Oslo the next morning, yet more news was breaking, this time out of London: singer Amy Winehouse was dead. A drug overdose was suspected. Terror attacks in Oslo, Australian history at the Tour de France, and a dead superstar equalled three major world stories all at the same time. Any one of them could have led the news agenda, but terror in Europe was the major headline. We stayed in Oslo.

•

The day before, the killer had stood over his victims with a frightening calm. He was emotionally detached from humanity and spared no mercy for the lives he was taking. One day he was an ordinary citizen; the next he was a cold-blooded executioner. He raised his rifle at a cowering teenager, paused for a moment, and then pulled the trigger. Another innocent life was lost but many more were to come.

The man was tall, with pale white skin, blond hair and blue eyes. Nordic in the classical sense. His name was Anders Behring Breivik. He was a 32-year-old with a deranged political score to settle.

Two hours earlier, Breivik had begun his bloodthirsty rampage when he parked a Volkswagen van loaded with 1100 kilograms of explosives, made from a mixture of fuel and fertiliser, outside the Oslo offices of Norway's Prime Minister Jens Stoltenberg. The blast from the car bomb was so big and powerful that it smashed the windows of the government offices and left rubble and glass scattered over the streets. Smoke rose into the summer air as fire burned inside the building.

Traumatised Australian expat Daniel Cherubini described the attack to me when I met him at the blast site the following day. He was a few blocks away at the time of the explosion but still felt its incredible force. 'That shock hit me and it hasn't left me. We heard a large explosion. We heard a sound and a massive shockwave hit us. All the glass everywhere shattered around us. It was quite scary.'

Eight people were killed in the attacks on the government buildings, and more than 200 people were injured. But that was only the first part of Breivik's plan. Part two was much more devastating.

Breivik drove 40 kilometres northwest of Oslo to a ferry on the Tyrifjorden. He was dressed in a police uniform and was armed with a pistol and an automatic rifle. He told the ferry driver that he needed to be transported to the nearby

Utøya Island, where a summer youth camp organised by the country's ruling Labour Party was being held. He apparently told the driver that he needed to get to the island and brief the students about the attacks in Oslo. Utøya is a peaceful, beautiful island with lush green trees and grass, surrounded by glassy calm waters. The kind of waters you could skip stones across. As Breivik was making the short trip across the lake to the small island, a group of boys and girls who had heard the explosions in Oslo gathered at the shore. They saw columns of smoke rise in the distance and could only wonder what had happened. Some of them had received calls on their mobile phones about the blasts. They couldn't have known that the man who was responsible was closing in on them fast.

When he came ashore, the killing spree began. Breivik calmly fired his weapons indiscriminately. The innocent young political activists had been amongst friends, playing games and sharing ideas, but now they were running for their lives. Breivik hunted them down. In a short space of time, dead bodies were sprawled out on the ground, but Breivik wanted more victims.

At this stage, the authorities were still struggling to deal with the original attacks in the city, and were busy cordoning off streets. It would be almost an hour before specialist SWAT teams were dispatched to the island following reports of gunshots. Breivik had had a decent head start and made the most of every free minute. He paced through the trees and fired so-called dum dum bullets, which are designed to expand inside the body and cause maximum tissue damage. The young boys and girls hid wherever they could. Some lay under mattresses, others ran down steep hills and cowered behind trees. A few more were chased down to the water's edge. Breivik spotted some on the shore, walked towards them, and fired more gunshots. Ammunition wasn't a problem because he was armed to the teeth. Some of the kids had no choice but to dive into the cold water and swim away. But anyone who has swum fully clothed knows how difficult that can be. The clothes become heavy and weigh you down, and it's easy to drown. Some brave souls did manage to get away, including a fourteen-year-old boy, but as others came up for air they were shot dead.

Other victims played dead. Several have since claimed they wouldn't be alive otherwise. Pretending to be dead on the ground, and as blood seeped from their wounds, they had to make sure their chests wouldn't visibly rise and fall. Several told media outlets afterwards that they could hear the crackle of Breivik's boots against the stony ground. One of the survivors quoted in my report said, 'I was lying perfectly still and one [victim] fell down right in front of me so I hid behind that person. I could hear him breathe and could hear his boots while he was walking.'

According to witnesses, Breivik remained cool throughout the shooting spree. Not once did he bristle. There was a rage inside him that had been building for years, and now it was being cruelly released. According to survivors his face remained calm, although some said he smiled on occasion before he squeezed the trigger. Another survivor who featured in my reports said, 'He was really relaxed. There was no stress. Nothing. It was like it was something he usually did. Like this was normal.'

Breivik's killing spree lasted close to an hour before he was cornered near a patch of forest on the island. He tossed his guns to the side and calmly fell to the ground where police arrested him. Game over. What started with a bomb blast at 3.26 pm ended with the killer's arrest at 6 pm. The guns fell silent, and the grief set in.

Some of the survivors lost limbs and were permanently disfigured from the gunshots, and even those who weren't hit suffered deep mental scarring. But they were the lucky ones. They were alive. Dozens never made it off the island. Young people with their lives ahead of them would never achieve their hopes and dreams. Sixty-nine people were killed on Utøya, as well as the eight who died in Oslo. Norway would never be the same again.

One of the things about this story that irritated me editorially was that many networks refused to call it a terror attack. Because Breivik was white it was just a mass shooting. I believed then, as I do now, it was a terror attack because by its definition terror means extreme fear. Extreme fear was felt by the Norwegians in the city of Oslo and the poor kids on Utøya Island because of Breivik's actions; therefore Breivik was a terrorist, proving not all terrorists are Muslims.

•

The day after the attacks, I was standing on the edge of the lake, looking across at Utøya Island, where black body bags were being loaded onto a boat for transportation to the morgue. It was an overcast day, to match a mood of misery. I was looking at the scene of one of the worst mass shootings by a solo gunman that the world has known. We weren't allowed to report from the island because it was a crime scene, but from a distance of a few hundred metres I could see the police tape and the officers in flak jackets moving from each individual piece of evidence to the next.

A beautiful country had lost its innocence at the hands of a deranged lunatic. On the edge of the lake, candles burned in memory of the victims, while people placed flowers and formed makeshift shrines. Other people did what I did. They just stood and looked in sombre silence. There isn't anything more silent than silence but in the aftermath of a terror strike the silence is deafening because it's so eerie and awful to perceive.

Norwegians are a very reserved people. It's their nature to quietly go about their business. The small crowds who were outdoors walked with their eyes fixed on the pavement. There weren't many cars on the road. Usually bustling restaurants and pubs were empty. People were in a state of shock. Terror has that effect.

The mood in Norway was perfectly summed up during Breivik's first court appearance a few days later. I was in court, along with many members of the world's media, before it was decided that it would be a closed session. No media access was granted. I thought it was a strange decision considering the size of the case and the international interest, but perhaps the authorities were concerned about the welfare of victims who had come to see the face of the killer. I walked back downstairs to the street and waited for the police van to arrive with their prized catch inside. I wasn't the only one. Hundreds of Norwegians lined the streets, waiting. It was one of the most interesting things I have ever seen. People stood in lines on the street, and they stood in silence, just as they had done all week. I felt strange talking to the camera, reporting on the events for Nine's national news bulletins, because there were so many people around me but no one else was saying a thing.

Gradually we learned more and more about Breivik and his motives. He lived alone in a rural property outside Oslo, and had planned the attack for years. He was a far right-wing terrorist; a self-confessed fascist who held a deep-seated hatred towards Islam, and was strongly opposed to multiculturalism. At a pre-trial hearing he called the government and its future members traitors who were guilty of cultural genocide. In a 1500-page manifesto that was published online ninety minutes before the first attack, Breivik wrote about his violent plans and how to construct bombs. He was an active member of a shooting club and was addicted to violent video games, including

'World of Warcraft'. He called himself a member of the Knights Templar.

It was hard for people to stomach Breivik's rantings while they grieved – all those sickening details involving so much anger and hatred. People rightfully asked the question, 'How did the police not see it coming?' But blame would come later; before that it was time for mourning.

I covered the first of the funerals, which was also attended by Prime Minister Stoltenberg and the Norwegian royal family. It was dominated by a huge floral tribute outside the cathedral and thousands of people who lined the funeral route. They couldn't get inside the church but just being there was enough. That was just one funeral; there were another seventy-six afterwards.

In August 2012, more than a year after the attacks, Anders Behring Breivik was sentenced to twenty-one years in prison – the maximum term in Norway. But because his crimes were so severe, and he never showed any remorse, it's unlikely he will ever be released. According to Norwegian law, if someone is regarded as a danger to society then they cannot be allowed back outside.

•

I have a few framed newspaper front pages hanging on my wall from papers in the United States, the United Kingdom, mainland Europe and the Middle East. They cover various big stories that I have reported over the years, and now serve as mementos or keepsakes. They remind me of the good and evil in life and are sometimes more powerful than photographs. One of them, in fact my favourite one, is from Norway. It shows a picture of a six-year old child named Nora who is sitting on the shoulders of her father. She's holding a red rose in the air. It's such a simple gesture; a salute to the dead. Little Nora was one of 150,000 people who stood in the main street of Oslo and thrust a white or red rose above their heads in honour of Breivik's victims.

I was there. It was less than a week after the attacks, and a huge crowd had gathered in the capital. It was the biggest rally in Norway since World War II. I stood and watched as people defiantly gathered in the open, unafraid of a repeat attack. They were ready to be outdoors again, they were ready to let go, and they were in full voice. The people were defending democracy and lambasting terrorism – not with violence or aggression, but with a rose and its thorny stalk.

For me, that image of a single rose raised into the air was as powerful as the body bags of Utøya. Nora represented the innocence of Norway, and the rose in the air was a nod to the future. While things can never be forgotten, there is always hope that better days are ahead.

Chapter 5

THE BLACK FLAG

THE ISLAMIC STATE IN IRAQ AND SYRIA ──────

It's just a flag. A black flag. That's all it is. A piece of fabric fluttering in the breeze. Yet what it stands for is terrible. Executions, crucifixions, mass murder, beatings, stonings, hangings, rape, terrorism – all that is horrible in the world committed under the black banner of the so-called Islamic State (IS).

It was 7 September 2014 and we were south of Kirkuk, on the road to Tikrit – the birthplace of former Iraqi dictator Saddam Hussein. Many people in the region wished he was still alive. We were travelling on a dry, dusty road heading to an isolated compound where Kurdish fighters of the Kurdistan Workers' Party (known as PKK) military group were based. Dozens of armed fighters, men and women, were bunkered down and, at the time, keeping Islamic militants at bay. Then we passed it. The flag. Raised high on a pole by the side of the road.

'That's it,' said our fixer Fazel Hawramy. We were now in IS territory. As Western journalists, James and I would no doubt be high-value targets. They would call us infidels and demand a ransom from the Australian government, which in all likelihood wouldn't come. Then they would parade us in front of the cameras, execute us in cold blood, and claim it to be in response to our military intervention; if we were caught, that is. Not many Westerners were in the region anymore. Western journalists and aid workers had been beheaded under sickening circumstances, which, quite rightly, frightened many away. American freelance journalist Steven Sotloff, who had been kidnapped in Syria a year earlier, had just been killed. He was paraded by black-clad militants and beheaded on camera by a fighter known as Jihadi John. We had filed a story on the gruesome death a few nights earlier from Erbil in northern Iraq.

So there we were, driving slowly south, without making much of a sound. The only noise was of tyres rolling over the bitumen, and the hot air blowing through the slightly open windows. The tension was palpable. The flag had triggered an anxiety in all of us. I'd seen it on television screens, and in newspapers or online, where militants held it proudly aloft. It was usually accompanied by a severed head. I felt uneasy but tried to keep my concerns locked inside my mind. I had been attracted to a story I'd seen in the local paper about a group of female fighters who were on the frontlines. I wanted to tell their story and Fazel knew how to get to them.

We were following another vehicle that was taking us to the PKK compound. Our English security guard, Russ, was tense. Whenever the leading car moved too far in front of us he would bark at our driver. 'Don't let them get too far away. I don't trust him.' Trust was important and dangerous in equal measure in the region at the time.

We found the compound in the middle of the desert, about 260 kilometres north of Baghdad, and about 100 kilometres south of Erbil. It could have been no-man's-land. In many ways, it was. A few soldiers manned the compound's entrance, with AK-47s slung over their shoulders. Fazel's contact had negotiated our admission, and the fighters seemed pleased to see us. But trust is not so easily earned. While we were unsure of the men and women in the compound, they were equally suspicious of us.

Just like in Libya, James and I were taken to a room for a little talk. Shoes off. Camera left at the door. Manners essential. They sat us down on a patterned rug in the middle of the room. There was no sign of the women yet, just the men, who were hospitable. They were dressed in army fatigues and looked like they'd been there a while. We were offered a cup of tea, which was not unusual. Then came the questions. 'Who are you?' 'Who do you work for?' 'What do you want?' Standard questions which came with standard answers. I said through Fazel, 'We work for Channel Nine Australia. We want to film a story here on your female fighters against IS. Very brave, eh?' A nod and slight smiles washed over the bearded faces of our hosts. A look that suggested they were proud of their sisters in arms. It was early afternoon and time was getting away. We needed to get back to Erbil before it was too dark, so I wouldn't have much time to speak to the women. The men interviewed us for a while longer, and we even laughed a little, before they gave us the okay.

They led us to another small concrete building where the women were waiting. They had been talking and quietly laughing to themselves. The mood was very relaxed. It was at complete odds with the situation I thought we were in. I was intrigued to learn that IS positions were about 400 metres away. 'Four hundred metres?' I asked. 'Yes,' the eldest of the group replied. She pointed to an area off in the barren distance. We peeked over the high dirt wall that protected the compound. The haze that bounced off the bright sand meant it was difficult to see exactly where she was referring to so I took her word for it. Who was I to argue? There were about a dozen women in the group aged between eighteen and fifty but they were sheepish about giving away too many details, including their names. Fair enough. They could have been doing anything else but instead they chose to work with a trigger and the barrel of a gun. It was their version of serving justice, they told me; justice for the women being raped and kept as slaves by extremists across their homeland. Their courage and their enthusiasm were to be admired. '[The extremists] are just thugs and they need to be stopped,' the leader told me.

The irony was that the PKK was considered a terrorist organisation by several Western states and NATO. For more than thirty years, the left-wing militant group has waged an armed struggle against governments in Turkey and Iraq because of what it claims are repressive regimes. They fight independently of the Kurdish Peshmerga forces, which are the official military forces of Iraqi Kurdistan. Splintered groups were not uncommon in the region at the time. Different fighters were all pitched against the common enemy of IS.

All things considered, the compound was a decent size, about the length and width of a football field. It contained a few small concrete sheds for sleeping, and self-made lookout towers where fighters kept watch. As I walked along the boundary, on the inside of a high wall made of sand, one of the women told me that surprise attacks were regular. It had been quiet for a few days though. They hadn't needed to kill anyone. I asked if they were vulnerable to attacks at night, when visibility was poor, because I couldn't see much in the way of modern combat equipment – just loads of guns and armoured vehicles. Maybe that was all that was needed. The other side probably didn't have much more. The female fighter smiled and told me there were many PKK fighters patrolling the compound at all hours in the armoured vehicles and their numbers were greater than those who fought under the black flag. We were a long way from the hotbed of extremist activity in north-eastern Syria and north-western Iraq, so the local IS may not have been as strong, but they were there, and it was still dangerous.

The sun was starting to drop. We needed to get back to Erbil, which was a few hours drive away, before dark, so we said thanks and left.

After the intensity of the road trip in, the story itself was an anti-climax. Although I was impressed with the bravery of these women, and the intelligence of the frontline fighters, it was the flag that left a lasting impression on me.

Historians tell us that the origins of the black flag date back to the days of the Prophet Muhammad, whose own flag was of a black square made of striped wool. In William McCants's book *The ISIS Apocalypse*, he says that when the caliphate was born, 'The commander of the faithful [Abu Umar al-Baghdadi] issued his decree, informed by knowledgeable people, that the flag of the IS is black.'

The Arabic lettering on the flag is the Muslim profession of faith. At the top of the black flag 'There is no god but Allah [God]' is scrawled in white print, while 'Muhammad is the messenger of God' is written in black inside a white circle, which is meant to resemble the prophet's seal.

But it wasn't the look of the flag that I was thinking about as I stared out the window of the cramped car on the long drive north back to Erbil. What the flag meant was the real kicker for me. That black fabric united the most brutal terror group of the modern age. It was not just the symbol of IS's movement in Iraq and Syria, and of its self-proclaimed caliphate; according to IS leadership it represented the Islamic army as it readied for a final battle to mark the end of days.

•

The West – led by the United States, and including Australia – helped create the so-called Islamic State. Or, rather, we created the power vacuum that allowed the terror group to grow. We can try to deny that all we like, but it just ain't no use. To the best of my knowledge, this is the short version of the story.

Islamic State foundations were laid in Iraq during and after the second Gulf War, which started in 2003, and the failed search for the weapons of mass destruction. The US military set up a detention centre on the Iraq–Kuwait border, which became known as Camp Bucca. More than 100,000 prisoners were funnelled through the centre and the result was that some of the most extreme and dangerous detainees were brought together, including jihadis and former members of Saddam Hussein's military, security and intelligence services. At the camp, they met and planned. The wheels for retaliation were in motion.

When Saddam was toppled as Iraq's leader in April 2003, the US dissolved the Iraqi army and removed those who were politically aligned with Saddam. This meant that thousands of jobs belonging to Sunni Muslims were taken away. Not surprisingly, they became disaffected and held a mighty grudge.

By around 2007, plans were in place for a new Islamic caliphate. Its leadership, then fronted by a chap named Abu Bakr al-Baghdadi, tried and failed to establish one in Yemen, then Mali, and then Somalia. For a variety of reasons they didn't work. They were broken up by Western forces and could never gain popular support from the public. Then came the chaos of the Arab Spring in 2011.

After watching the successful revolutions in Libya and Egypt, Syrians were keen to reclaim their civil rights and freedoms too. But rather than quash the uprising, beleaguered President Bashar al-Assad stirred the pot and eventually played a strong hand in helping IS create an army. According to reports, as peaceful protests began in northern parts of Syria, the Assad regime released about 260 jihadis from prison. A volatile land became a breeding ground for extremists. Even more disturbingly, online forums about the situation in Syria attracted fanboys from all over the world. As the years passed and the Syrian civil war rumbled on, IS quietly became stronger by attracting thousands of new soldiers made up of Sunni allies and disgruntled tribesmen. Those former Saddam loyalists and officers from Bucca prison could train up a new generation of fighters and military strategists. To borrow an old cliché, it was a perfect storm.

In early 2014, the beast was let out of the cage. The IS army crossed the border from Syria into Iraq and with lightning speed and primitive brutality it conquered Iraq's second city of Mosul. Any Iraqi soldiers who stood in their way were murdered in cold blood. Thousands of Iraqis were shot, beheaded, hanged, and buried in mass graves. Why was IS so violent? Because extreme violence brought attention to the propaganda machine. Extreme violence, fear, and terror became the hallmarks of the new Islamic State. Iraqi soldiers quickly learned about the storm that was coming so they fled for their lives, which is why IS was able to seize so much ground in those early days. And here's the thing that makes Islamic State extremists so powerful and frightening – they have no fear of death.

●

'Remember, you wanted to be here,' my producer Wes Hardman had said to me the first time I flew into Baghdad. There was a cheeky smile on his face as he peered over the seat; a friendly reminder that if something happened it wasn't anybody's fault but my own. So I laughed, nervously, and then returned my gaze to the window as a hot blast of sun warmed my face. Wes was right. I wanted to be in Baghdad. I'd always wanted to report from Iraq. I was too young to be part of the Gulf wars, and could only watch on television as history's great journalists reported from the desert during the nineties and noughties. But it was June 2014 and Islamic State fighters were closing in on the Iraqi capital, having already conquered many key towns and villages across the country. It was my chance to report from Baghdad.

We were on a Royal Jordanian flight from Amman to the Iraqi capital. The plane had aged and there was a hospital gurney at the back of it to transport anyone who needed immediate medical attention. That was an unsettling sight. Both Wes and our cameraman, Ben Williamson, had been to Iraq before, but it was my first time and I wasn't sure what to expect. Wes had seen everything and spoken to everyone over the years and knew a hell of a lot about the intricacies, complications, and rich history of the Middle East, so having him with me was a pretty good start.

In 2014, the only things that seemed to talk in Baghdad were money and permits – and the two often went hand in hand. Filming permits cost thousands of dollars, and different permits were needed for different areas. The only television crews who roamed wherever they liked were the ones who were permanently based in the city – and by then there weren't many of those. We decided to take a punt without a permit. Just getting an Iraqi visa had been difficult enough, and it was only secured by Wes's charm back in Amman. We figured we'd manage without a permit. We were mistaken.

Before we even got out of the Baghdad International Airport, our entire broadcasting equipment was confiscated by airport security. No camera, no tripod, no sound gear, no lights. No good for television news. We were escorted to a separate storage facility a short drive away where Ben had to sign away his equipment. I waited in our armoured four-wheel drive, wondering how the heck we were going to do any work now. Never mind security concerns, if we couldn't broadcast our stories there was basically no point being there.

I joined Wes outside the car as hot desert gusts blew across the barren earth. The air was thick and the temperature felt like it was in the high forties. Ben joined us with a disappointed look but it wasn't the end of the road. There was still a way to make it work. Sometimes a smartphone and a little internet access is all you need. Ben happened to have a high definition GoPro camera still in his possession. Broadcast quality. No one at home would know the difference. He'd slipped it past the guards, or maybe they just didn't think anything could be done with something so small. He also had a laptop computer and a separate sound recording device. It wasn't ideal but it was enough to get us by. So as we travelled from the airport into the city, he filmed our journey.

We sped along Baghdad Airport Road, known as Route Irish, a twelve-kilometre road that linked the airport to the heavily fortified Green Zone in the centre of the city where the international forces had been located. The highway was once the most dangerous stretch of road in the world. During the Iraq War it was a constant target for roadside bombs, suicide bombers, and drive-by shootings. Things had calmed down since then, but the city was still on edge. There were regular attacks from suicide bombers and car bombs, and Baghdad bore the scars of years at war. Soldiers patrolled just about every street corner and armed men at roadblocks searched every car that entered the city for bombs or explosive devices. Similar security measures were set up outside hotels. Without question, it was the most paranoid city I'd ever been to.

Baghdad is a tangled maze of built-up concrete homes and buildings, dirty streets of shops and food stores, blast walls that protect buildings from bombs, and dry parklands near the famous Tigris River. We stayed at a hotel with high security and a functioning restaurant. The city was not the kind of place you wanted to wander around at night looking for food. Over the next few days, we slipped out of the hotel to use broadcast equipment provided by local television facilities so we could file live reports back to Australia, but filming our own material for the news back home was tricky. Just to visit and film a story on an ordinary family living in the city required a thorough plan. Serious questions needed to be addressed, such as how to get there, how long to stay, and how to get back. And without an official permit, we were severely restricted in where we could go. Fortunately, we found a family who were happy with us sneaking into their small home. But we had to be fast. In any place of high tension, it's always best to work fast and not stay outside in public areas for too long.

It was sketchy enough for Ben and me to walk out of the hotel and a few hundred metres to Firdos Square where the statue of Saddam Hussein once stood before it was torn down by a mob in what became the defining image of the Iraq War. I stood in the square and watched as old sedans and taxis circled the roundabout. As Ben and I briefly filmed a sequence, I thought how naive we must have looked. A couple of Westerners standing alone in a troubled city. We continued to take our chances by filming on the GoPro. We almost lost the camera though when a paranoid security team didn't like us filming cars being checked for bombs near a block of apartments. Ben had to tell them we deleted the pictures, which we didn't. We became terribly possessive over the smallest things we managed to film.

At the time, Baghdad was a prize that Islamic State wanted. But, unlike Iraq's second city of Mosul in the north-west, it was not such a simple land grab. The capital was the heartbeat of the nation, home to more than seven million people and the base of Iraq's military machine, so it was extremely well protected. Militants landed devastating punches through random bombings at shopping centres and markets, but no one had been able to deliver a knockout blow. In June 2014, however, groups of IS fighters were close enough to be considered a serious threat. They had already seized about 70 per cent of the Anbar Province to Baghdad's west. While we were in the capital, small groups of militant fighters got to within 20 kilometres of the airport, and dozens of civilians were killed after a handful of car bombs were ignited south of the city. It made for a cagey environment and our movement was severely hampered.

Eventually we were pulled out of the capital. Our news editors back in Sydney must have thought it wasn't worth the expense. I don't blame them. On the ground, we were frustrated because our attempts to work were stifled by a paranoid army and a lack of permits. At those times, I really envied print journalists because they could stay under the radar a lot better than we could. Cameras tend to stand out. But we were happy enough with what we had been able to do under the circumstances, and by providing live reports daily from the capital we were able to inform our viewers about what was happening in the region. Baghdad was done for now, but Iraq wasn't. I would be back, and very soon.

•

'Get out of the car. Move!' Russ, our security consultant, shouted at us from the front seat. The small sedan we were travelling in had screeched to a stop and our bodies lunged forward. We were held up by another vehicle that had stopped at a checkpoint. Our security had seen something. 'Out, out, out,' he demanded.

Luke Wilson and I had our armour on so it wasn't the smoothest or the fastest exit. Friggin' flak jackets. We got out and bolted off the road and over a mound of dirt, which we hid behind in case bullets started flying. We peered over the edge of the rocky brown earth, and then looked back to where we'd come from, taking deep breaths because of the heavy load we were carrying. About 20 metres away a man in military fatigues was holding his pistol in the air and seemed to be threatening to shoot. Luke skilfully filmed half-a-dozen men who were shouting at each other in Arabic. It was a tense standoff. Neither of us had any idea what was going on because our translator had bolted in the other direction. Handy. Moments passed, and then the vocal decibels dropped. The sticking point was no more. No one was shot. Not here, anyway. We piled back into the car with slightly slower heartbeats and carried on with our journey.

It was 6 September 2014; we had just passed the north-western Iraqi township of Kalak and were on our way to Mosul, which IS had claimed as its headquarters. Well, we were on our way to an area that was on the outskirts of Mosul. We weren't idiots, although sometimes it might seem that way. Who would want to go anywhere near the base of the world's most feared terror group? I guess we did, although we felt like the odds were in our favour because of who we were with. I had become friendly with some members of the Kurdish Peshmerga forces – the only army in Iraq that had stood its ground while Islamic militants surged deep into Iraqi territory a few months prior. Our sedan was part of a small motorcade of vehicles transporting senior members of the Peshmerga along with a few other cars containing some local journalists. The Australian government was sending weapons and ammunition to the Peshmerga to help them out, so we were there to follow the trail. Plus, the Peshmerga were grateful that we were telling their story.

One of the Peshmerga fighters had given us a tip-off that a crucial hill about 30 kilometres outside Mosul had just been retaken by Peshmerga forces. Hills are strategically important because they allow whoever is on them to survey the areas below and, in daylight hours, potentially see any advances. It's Warfare 101. Find the higher ground.

Not long after our drama at the checkpoint, we veered left onto a dirt track. Our security man was in the front passenger seat. Luke and I were squeezed in to the back of the small sedan, which was very low to the ground. We felt every bump and sway. We heard every crack and pop. The car would be buggered after this. Dust was kicked up from the car in front of us but we didn't want to fall too far behind in case there was a surprise attack.

We drove across dry dusty paddocks, up and down hills and through open farmland until we eventually came to a small village that was perched on the side of a larger hill, almost a mountain. There was IS graffiti on the walls of houses and on the sides of the road to signify their presence. The fact that the village had obviously been emptied in a hurry made that clear anyway.

We slowly drove along the dirt streets, past a few dozen homes. Chickens had been let out of cages, and a few goats walked along the side of the track. I wondered what things they had seen.

We continued further up the hill to where the Peshmerga fighters had massed. There must have been more than a hundred of them, all armed to the teeth with Kalashnikovs, assault rifles, pistols, and rocket-propelled grenade launchers. I didn't feel like it was an especially tense environment though. A few dozen of them chatted and laughed to themselves, like anyone else at the end of a good day. They were pleased with what they claimed was a small victory. They told me the bodies of seven IS fighters were left at the top of the hill. They'd been killed in a fierce battle earlier in the day and had been left there as a warning. The rest of the IS militants had fled back to wherever they'd come from. There were a few villages between the hill and Mosul so it was assumed the militants had disappeared into them.

A Peshmerga soldier showed me a couple of old mobile phones that had wires poking out of them. IS militants had planted them in the village's houses before they fled. They were small black mobile devices that looked a bit like the first Nokia phones. They were the trigger for a bomb, I was told. It was hard to argue with that.

We didn't have much time. The hill was strategically important and the militants would no doubt want it back. The sun only had a few hours left. So, sticking to my theory of never staying out in the open for too long, we filmed our piece as quickly as we could.

The hill was actually a beautiful setting. Blue skies and rolling hills, dirt roads and stunning views, but the farmlands below were now the badlands. I wondered if you could see Mosul from the top of the hill. Mosul – the city I, along with much of the world, had heard plenty about recently.

According to those who had escaped the city, IS held absolute power over Mosul's residents at the time and was enforcing an extreme interpretation of Islamic law. Women were forced into sexual slavery, rape was actively encouraged, and anyone who refused to follow IS orders was killed. Punishments and executions were performed in public to serve as a warning to others. Someone could be whipped or flogged with a power cable just for smoking a cigarette. Theft was punished by the amputation of a hand. If a man committed adultery, or was believed to be gay, he was thrown off a building; a woman was stoned to death. It was a bleak existence.

Mosul was well fortified because the IS fighters had taken weapons, ammunition, and hardware from Iraqi and Syrian military bases and also from fleeing soldiers. IS had also amassed a lot of money through bank robberies, oil trade and ransom payments.

Everyone was talking about Mosul at the time, so Luke and I decided to head up to the top of the hill to see if we could film the city from a distance. It was a rocky, steep terrain with trees and shrubs, and it would have taken us a good half hour to walk, which was an issue so late in the day. But we hadn't even properly begun our trek before we were stopped. There was a deep boom in the distance. The unmistakeable dull thud that I'd heard many times before. I couldn't tell if the rockets were incoming or outgoing, but I counted three of them in relatively quick succession. 'They're coming,' I was told by a Peshmerga soldier. 'You'd better go.' The militants either wanted revenge for their dead comrades or, more likely, they wanted the hill back. We already had enough material to file a strong story and, even though I wanted to take a peek at Mosul from the top of the hill, there was no real incentive to stick around. Not so close to Mosul. So we piled into our little sedan and left.

I'd paid our driver a few hundred dollars to drive us several hours each way from Erbil to the edge of Mosul, and he hadn't complained. But I saw the pained look on his face as the car started rattling during our hasty exit. His brakes were shot, and his suspension cracked at every bump and turn. I hoped the sedan would get us back in time. We snaked our way back along the desert. I looked behind and saw a satellite truck for the local TV reporters who were with us following our trail, which made me laugh. It would have been doing it tougher than us.

Once we returned to the bitumen highway the car was all right, and the driver breathed a sigh of relief. When we got back to the hotel in Erbil I gave him more than enough cash to fix his car, which included a tip for taking us where we had to go, and a few extra dollars for any nervousness he might have felt.

Later I was told that IS militants did try to repossess the hill, but were foiled by the Peshmerga again.

•

A few days after our trip to the hill, I was talking to a man named Younis Muhammad, who looked defeated. Maybe he was just tired, or hungry, or both. His body was lying to him about his age, he told me. He was forty-four yet he felt much older. He couldn't stand because his legs wouldn't carry him any further. Dressed in a dirt-stained *thawb* – a long-sleeved, ankle-length robe – and well-worn sandals, he reached out to shake my hand. A humble gesture from a humble man.

As a tractor driver in the Iraqi countryside, Younis thought he knew the meaning of a hard life. Then IS came to town. Younis lived to the north of Mosul with his wife, two young sons and daughter. When IS militants swept in, those townspeople who refused to be cast under its spell joined a great migration out of there. The family walked nearly 100 kilometres to a refugee camp just outside Erbil. During their two-day trek, temperatures were upwards of 50 degrees as they dragged themselves through dry, windswept desert. There were no road signs to safety, no advertising boards or banners, just a long straight road east. They couldn't be sure that militants wouldn't intercept them.

Younis and his family reached safety at the Baharka tent city, which is where I found them. They were resting under the shade of a tent, which had been provided by the United Nations Refugee Agency (UNHCR). Despite the long and tiring journey, Younis was eager to share his story and the grievances he felt towards the IS militants who had upended his life.

'They took everything from us. We left our house, and we left our belongings. Everything was there. But the worst part for me was seeing my wife and children cry.'

Younis knew how lucky he was to have his young family with him. The UNHCR had built 10,000 tents at Baharka and they were lined up in neat rows along the dry ground. The family ate and slept together inside one of the small canvas tents, which had slim mats rolled out on its hard floor. It was shelter, but hot wind gusts blew huge walls of brown sand in from the desert and coated everything in their path. Younis hadn't earned much money before – maybe a few dollars a day – but now he earned nothing because he'd had to leave his job behind as well. Fortunately, most things were provided at Baharka – water, basic medical supplies and food, including bread and rice. There were communal male and female showers, and taps to collect water. The kids played in the puddles because there wasn't much else to do. If that's what made them laugh, then let them be.

Younis said he thought about his home constantly. Everything he had worked for was there. He thought about his village and his old friends. He had so many questions that would remain unanswered for a long time. What was left of his home? Of his friends? Of Mosul? He had no intention of going back home until IS was defeated, so Younis knew he might be stuck in the tent city for many months, possibly years.

The story of Younis Muhammad is not uncommon. All I had to do was step outside his tent and I was faced with 10,000 other people with similar stories.

And the 10,000 stories of Baharka are just a drop in the proverbial ocean. The Syrian war, and the ISIS advance, triggered the worst refugee crisis since World War II. Hundreds of thousands of lives have been lost, and millions more have been displaced.

I visited several refugee camps throughout 2014, some much larger than Baharka. I travelled to the Zaatari camp in northern Jordan near the Syrian border, which at the time was the biggest refugee facility in the world and home to more than 100,000 Syrians. But so many people living together in such desperate circumstances was problematic. As in any big city, there was violence and prostitution. Groups of people protested against the poor living conditions. I met one man who told me he would rather go back to war-torn Syria because the camp's basic supplies of water, bread, and shelter were not enough.

At Zaatari, I met Roger Hearn, the Australian head of the local Save the Children organisation, who gave me a tour of the huge sprawling desert camp, which even had its own dusty streets. We saw a makeshift kindergarten where dozens of children had gathered to learn and find some semblance of a normal life.

'We've seen some children who have stopped talking,' Roger said, 'and they've stopped talking for a good deal of time because they're so traumatised. At some of those siege areas we've heard about from inside Syria, children have actually had to walk over dead bodies to get out and get to safety.'

It wasn't the first time I had heard stories of children suffering in the conflict. Before IS declared a caliphate in June 2014, I had tried to get into the Syrian capital, Damascus, via Beirut in Lebanon. It was just after sickening images emerged of children frothing at the mouth after chemical weapons were used by the Syrian regime against its own people. It's still hard to watch: little bodies writhing on the floor as their parents cried out in a mixture of anger and despair. It had been the final straw for the West. US President Barack Obama said that a red line had been crossed, and military hardware was moved into position along the Mediterranean.

James Gillings and I had sat in Beirut and waited for the rockets to fire over Lebanon and into Syria. But the statement had been an Obama misstep. Even though he said a red line had been crossed, what was he going to do? The Syrian conflict had become a proxy war. If the US and its allies attacked Syria, then Russia, Iran, Lebanon, and Israel would be dragged in and World War III would have surely begun.

I filed visa applications at the Syrian border, but the only TV crews who were allowed into Syria legally were those who represented major networks from the United States and Britain. They were granted access to President Assad who used them as a mouthpiece.

Instead of entering Syria, I visited another refugee camp on the border between Syria and Lebanon. Sadly, it was more of the same. Adults who had carried a weight that's far beyond anything most of us could ever imagine, and children who had seen things that couldn't be unseen.

•

Rowsch Shaways was an interesting fellow. As the former Deputy Prime Minister of Iraq, he knew a thing or two about the region and its politics. The IS advance was the biggest crisis he'd faced in years. When I met him in September 2014, he was aged in his late sixties and based in northern Iraq where he was helping facilitate the weapons exchanges from foreign governments to the Kurdish Peshmerga forces.

We were based in Erbil, the capital of the Kurdish region of Iraq. It's much more beautiful than Baghdad, and is famous for a huge citadel that looks down on the city, which has been around since about 2300 BC. It's now World Heritage listed.

Erbil was much easier to fly into and out of than Baghdad. No gear was confiscated, no permits were needed, and so there were no restrictions on movement. We decided where we wanted to go, a decision that was based on safety.

The city was relatively safe, but in the weeks before our arrival a few car bombs had exploded in town, which meant the usually busy markets were quiet. Dozens of IS sympathisers were arrested following further attempts to carry out attacks. But bombs within the walls of Erbil were much less frequent than the blasts in Baghdad. It was only when you ventured out of Erbil that risk increased.

I was at a military command post on the city's edge where journalists were able to meet representatives of the army and its commanders. It was how I came across Mr Shaways. He gave long and considered responses to questions I asked and he replied with a soft, thick accent.

'We are grateful for the weapons because we really need them,' he said.

After the interview, Mr Shaways's assistant took us for a drive so we could meet the frontline troops. The sun was setting as we travelled along a lonely stretch of highway until we came to a stop at a town called Gwer, which is about 30 kilometres south-west of Erbil. It was as far as we could go before we entered no-man's-land. We got out of the car and stood on the road. In the distance, at the foot of a mountain, I could see a village. 'ISIS is over there,' I was told, just a few kilometres away at a place called Kanash. All I could see were the white tops of cluttered homes and occasionally the headlights of a moving vehicle. No people or flags. It was too far away for that.

We got back in our four-wheel drive and sped off-road towards the Kurdish frontline where we arrived at supper-time. Dozens of moustached men in camouflaged military clothing sat around talking as they tucked into rice that was dished out on plastic plates. Some were drinking water, while others sipped tea. The mood was relaxed. Some of them even smiled and nodded to us as we said hello.

'Where you from?' we were asked. 'Australia,' we replied. 'Ahhh Australia, welcome.' It was always like that. Whatever place and whatever conflict I was in, I was generally made to feel welcome.

I stood on the edge of the bunker while Luke filmed the faces of the fighters and the surrounds of the frontline. I noticed that bullets had smashed some of the windows of armoured vehicles around us, evidence of a gun battle that had taken place prior to our arrival. 'We see their cars moving all the time,' I was informed. 'We can see where they go.' I was told by one of the commanders that sometimes the IS militants launched surprise counterattacks, but their most recent effort had been stifled by the bombs of American warplanes that landed in front of encroaching IS positions. The fire from the sky was a major advantage in the war. Well, out on the battlefield it was. In built-up areas the bombs were sometimes counterproductive because they forced militants to hide amongst civilians.

Since the bombs had forced them back, IS hadn't launched a new attack in several days. Apparently some of their soldiers were wounded. 'But it's best to be ready,' the Kurdish soldier said. I nodded in approval. It's always best to be ready, I thought, because this battle isn't over. It's not over by a long shot.

Chapter 6

THE PRICE OF FREEDOM

WAR IN UKRAINE

There is an old Latin phrase that reads, 'Laws fall silent in times of war.' In May 2014, in eastern Ukraine, the decibels of war were peaking and I watched as the law didn't just fall silent, it was chased out of town.

•

It was 8 May 2014 and it had been an otherwise uneventful day in the southern port city of Mariupol, before a few Russian-backed separatists were detained by police and taken down to the local station. What for? I never knew. But at that point it didn't really matter. Tensions had been building for weeks and the whole country was incredibly volatile as it slipped deeper into a civil war against Russian-backed separatists.

A mob of about a hundred people, fuelled by a mixture of rage and alcohol, weren't too happy about their friends being taken in, so they marched down to the station. The separatists wanted them back.

I was among the crowd, which was seething with rage, as they walked up to the gated police compound. The station was guarded by about two dozen armed police officers and they weren't in any mood for trouble. They raised their shotguns and aimed them at the civilian faces approaching them.

Young and middle-aged pro-Russians shook the steel gates of the front fence and shouted obscenities at the police. 'You filthy pigs!' one man said as he gesticulated wildly and pointed his finger at the armed officers less than ten metres in front of him. The barrel of a gun stared right back at him. It was an intense standoff and looked like it could turn very nasty very soon. Even the women were in on the action, shouting, 'Police scum! Give us back our boys!'

There were no other news crews around. It was just me, James Gillings, our British security consultant Tony, and our interpreter Mansur, a big burly Russian bloke with long hair that he wore tied back. Mansur was classic Russian. A fairly serious chap who was highly critical of the Russian regime – when he wasn't in Russia.

It was the middle of the day and the sun was beating down on us when I noticed a man who appeared to be a high-ranking officer emerge from the two-storey station block. Appearing pensive, he walked across the forecourt towards a few of the armed officers and whispered something in their ears. There was no obvious response to whatever instruction was given.

The shouting from the crowd was growing and their anger was at boiling point. Many of them threatened to jump the chest-high gates. I was close to the front of the pack and felt the tension rise as one of the armed officers moved even closer and raised his weapon towards us. It was already cocked, ready to fire. *Shit. He's going to shoot*, I thought.

Right at that point I realised that I'd become separated from James and Tony. They were about thirty metres away, off to the side between the two sets of opponents with an excellent vantage point to film whatever was about to come. But I was right where I was not supposed to be – in the middle of a screaming crowd who were almost asking to be shot.

Sure enough the crowd surged forward, and bullets pierced the air. CRACK. CRACK. CRACK. CRACK. I heard women scream as people crashed into each other, frantically trying to get away. Chaos breeds confusion and people scattered every which way. I didn't know what to do, so I quickly turned and took three or four giant leaps and threw myself headfirst into a grassy gully nearby – almost like a footballer diving for a tryline. I thought I was done for. CRACK. CRACK. CRACK. A few others dived over to where I was and hid. After a few manic moments, the gunshots stopped. Breathing heavily, I stayed down. I had no idea what had happened to the police or the people they were firing at and I was expecting to see a bloodbath.

After a while, I slowly peered over the edge of the gully and was again taken by surprise. Despite the gunfire, several men had stayed exactly where they were at the gate and continued to shout at the steely-looking officers even as guns were pointed right at their faces. Defiance. *Who were these people in custody?* I wondered. They must be hugely important to the separatist cause. Desperate times and desperate actions. Or maybe people were just looking for a fight.

A new wave of tension rolled in again, and I was still well away from James who was filming the whole thing. I needed to get to the camera to describe the scene that was unravelling, but I didn't know how. Right then I heard someone shouting my name, 'Peter! Peter!'

With dirt and sweat in my eyes, I peeked over the gully edge and tried to see where the voice was coming from. 'Peter!' I heard again in a British accent. It was Tony, our security consultant – a former SAS soldier who lived for this kind of rush. 'Get here now!' he commanded.

No way, I thought. Tony was next to James. To get to them I would have to run past the small crowd of separatists and across the line of sight of the armed cops. I was trapped. If I ran it would greatly increase my chances of getting shot.

The situation escalated again. There was screaming and shouting, and the police tossed some small canisters into the crowd to try and disperse them. At the time I wasn't sure whether the canisters were smoke or tear gas, but I felt I had to move – and fast. It seemed as though James was safe. The police could quite easily see it was a news camera he was holding and not a weapon. So I crawled over the edge of the gully, stood up, closed my eyes, held my breath and ran towards James and Tony.

It's an awful feeling waiting for a bullet to strike. My legs were like lead and each step felt like I was climbing a steep mountain. I tried to stay low as I quickly but carefully navigated my way through the cloud of smoke to get to James. It was only a short dash really, but it may as well have been a long one, and I couldn't help but wonder if I was on the radar of any of those policemen. I could have been anybody. How could they tell if I was a journalist or a separatist?

I finally made it to James. Aside from some dirt and grass stains down the front of my white shirt, I was unharmed. Like the professional he is, James was still filming and so Tony grabbed the microphone out of James's backpack and shoved it into my hand. Talk. When I jumped in front of the lens another canister landed near my feet and a plume of smoke rose into our shot.

As I described the uncertainty and the desperation of a police force under pressure, and the immense anger of the people at the station gate, a heavily armoured military vehicle arrived on the scene. Police had radioed for backup and it seemed things were about to shift another gear.

James and I dashed across the street and took cover near a red sedan. CRACK. CRACK. More gunshots were fired. As other people took shelter on different parts of the street, beads of sweat ran down my face.

I peered over the top of the red sedan and saw that some of the police had climbed into the armoured vehicle. A few of them were standing on top of it and pointing their barrels at the people below. One protester got right up into the face of a policeman on the ground who responded by smashing his rifle butt against the man's nose and busting it open.

The police were either outnumbered, or they feared another wave of protesters might arrive, so they were leaving.

The truck moved past our position and sped off down the street. Police had given up. Situation over.

Remarkably, no one had been killed, although there were a few injuries. I looked at the ground and saw bullet holes in the bitumen from where some of the shots had landed. Forty-five extremely tense minutes had wrapped up with a police evacuation, so we thought it best to leave.

As we climbed into our van, I looked back at the police station and saw two pro-Russian rebels waving from the top storey at a crowd who were now breaking in to get them.

They'd taken the law on, and run it out of town.

•

Kiev, Ukraine's capital, is a beautiful city, dominated by cobblestoned streets, fine architecture, old European buildings, and famous golden-domed cathedrals and monasteries, similar to those in neighbouring Moscow. Ukraine had once been part of the Soviet Union, and when the Iron Curtain crumbled down in 1991 it became its own independent state. But where there is beauty there is also a beast, which came in the form of a corrupt government led by President Viktor Yanukovych, who had long been regarded as a puppet of Russian President Vladimir Putin. The Russian president still thought of Ukraine as part of the Russian empire; he even referred to it as 'Little Russia'. It was claimed, by many, that the 2010 election that saw Yanukovych sweep to power was rigged and that Putin may have played a hand. Despite Ukraine's vast farming lands, rich gas and oil reserves, it was not a prosperous country. Its economy and currency had sputtered along at negative rates over the years because of financial mismanagement.

Towards the end of 2013, an eager generation of hopeful, educated students demanded Ukraine break free from the shackles of Russia so it could join the European Union. This would have opened up vital trade corridors with Western Europe and, in time, improved the nation's wealth and overall outlook. But by looking to the west, Ukraine would have had to turn its back on its long-time friend and neighbour, Russia. The people were so desperate for change, however, that they were willing to do anything to achieve it – even die. Just as we saw in the Middle East during the so-called Arab Spring of 2011, the youth were restless and now it was Ukraine's turn.

Yanukovych was in a pickle. His people were protesting about the poor state of Ukraine and the need to change it by joining the EU. At the same time, his friend Vladimir Putin, one of the most powerful men on the planet, wanted the two nations to stay tight. The pressure coming from both sides was immense.

Initially, President Yanukovych sided with the people. In December 2013 he announced an intention to sign an agreement, which would mean closer ties with the European Union. But at the eleventh hour he got the yips, and refused to do it. Instead of looking west, he turned east. The bullish Ukrainian leader defied the people and on 17 December 2013 signed a treaty with Russia, which included a multi-billion dollar loan deal. The treaty meant Russia could purchase up to 15 billion dollars worth of Ukrainian debt, and the cost of all natural gas supplied to Ukraine from Russia would almost be halved.

Rather than calm the protest movement and give in to their demands, Yanukovych's decision had a much more explosive result.

•

Independence Square in the centre of Kiev was the starting point for the new revolution. But the people had been there before. The circumstances were familiar.

Precisely nine years earlier, from November 2004 to January 2005, thousands of orange-clad people gathered to protest the aftermath of the 2004 Ukrainian Presidential election, in what became known as the Orange Revolution. The election had been marred by corruption, voter intimidation, and the poisoning of eventual winner Viktor Yushchenko of the Orange party, whose face was disfigured as a result of consuming a meal laced with dioxin. And you might have thought Australian politics was brutal! Coincidentally, Yanukovych was the candidate who lost.

Fast forward to the end of 2013. Yanukovych was in power. The cold winter months had set in, and Ukrainians were back at Independence Square. What had started as peaceful protests by candlelight developed into an occupation. After Yanukovych signed that deal guaranteeing closer ties with Russia in December 2013, more and more people carried their sleeping bags into the square and set up camp in front of the imposing Town Hall building and around a tall victory column, which was built in 2001 to mark the nation's independence. Most of the protesters came back and forth every day from their homes as if protesting was a job, but some slept on the concrete to make a point. Nights became weeks. Weeks became months. The snow started to fall, and soon a white blanket covered the ground. But every day the numbers grew. Hundreds of thousands of flag-waving protesters attended mass demonstrations. People set up tents and created little kitchens to serve food and drinks. It was a vibrant community of protest. But pretty soon it came crashing, or rather burning, down.

The Russian government apparently told its Ukrainian counterparts to come down hard on the rebellion and quash it, because it was embarrassing to both regimes. Order needed to be restored. In Russia, under Putin, public dissent was rarely accepted or even allowed – and Russia had almost always had a say in how Ukraine was run. The Russians may have thought to themselves, *This is why Ukraine needs the Russian Federation, because it can't even control its own people.*

The Ukrainian government first tried to disperse the crowds legally. In January 2014, Yanukovych's government dramatically passed tough anti-protest laws that meant jail time for anyone who continued to protest, whether it was peaceful or not. There was even an attempt to restrict internet access. The Ukrainian people saw it as a blatant attack on civil rights, and it wasn't accepted.

In the middle of January 2014, clashes between angry protesters and Ukraine's special police forces – called Berkut – became more brutal and more frequent. Police with truncheons bashed protesters on the streets. Picture that – a defenceless man lying on the snowy pavement, while several officers laid into him with kicks and punches, and bashed him with batons.

Dozens of people were killed, and many more were injured in the ensuing days. Order had well and truly broken down.

Kiev was suddenly a cauldron. Fire was burning from walls of tyres and blood was on the streets. The capital had become a very dangerous place. Masked defenders patrolled the camp sites and the protesters held their ground. Fearing reprisal, they set up barricades – planks of wood, sheets of iron, twisted metal, and tyres stacked high – around the perimeter of Independence Square. As expected, retaliation came hard and fast.

On 20 February 2014, after the first few billion dollars of Russian-backed bailout money was wired to Ukraine, an order came for the Berkut to crush the rebellion with force. The unconfirmed word was that Putin made the call.

From Washington, US President Barack Obama told reporters, 'We expect the Ukrainian government to show restraint. To not resort to violence in dealing with peaceful protesters.' He must have hoped his words would have a calming effect, but his plea went over like a damp squib.

Hundreds of government soldiers, including snipers, were sent in to deal with the crowd at Independence Square. At first they fired rubber bullets towards the protesters, but that didn't have much of an effect. So the rubber was quickly replaced with rounds of live ammunition. Many protesters were also armed and returned fire at government forces. Bullets pierced the air every which way. Most crashed into buildings but some of them tore through flesh, and men on both sides dropped to the ground. Some of the more industrious young protesters were lucky enough to have shields that had been stolen from riot police, and they also wore bike helmets for protection. The vision of the protesters and the government fighting was desperate and horrific.

I was in Sochi, the Russian resort town by the Black Sea, covering Australian athletes at the Winter Olympic

Games, when I saw images of ordinary citizens being shot on the streets. They slowly crept towards frontlines and suddenly dropped whatever they had, screamed in agony, and clutched at their legs or chests after they'd been hit. Some of the protesters just dropped to the ground without reacting – a life, with so much potential, gone in a flash. Dead bodies lay on the street. There were dozens of them. Some brave souls tried to rescue their wounded friends, but only got themselves killed in the act. More footage showed government snipers firing on their own people.

I couldn't believe that people were being killed like that in modern-day Europe. All of a sudden, after months of protests, Ukraine was teetering on the brink of civil war. Perhaps Putin thought his Sochi Olympics would distract the world's attention from what was going on in Kiev. It worked in the beginning, but when bodies started piling up, the world took notice.

The Winter Olympics were not going well for Australia, so it was quickly decided that I, alongside cameraman Luke Wilson, would move to the Ukrainian capital.

We headed to Moscow, where we applied for and collected our Ukrainian visas, which took twenty-four hours to receive. For a few thousand dollars we purchased body armour from a local dealer, which included bulletproof vests, helmets, and goggles for tear gas. With that, we flew to Ukraine just after it endured its most violent day since World War II. On 20 February 2014, seventy-seven people were gunned down on the streets, and more than a thousand protesters were wounded. It was a heartless, bloody-minded crackdown, and was heavily criticised by the global community. Ukraine was consumed by grief and despair. But it was just the start.

•

We arrived on 22 February 2014, two days after the massacre, and found a blackened battlefield of a city. Smoke rose from burning buildings, and a murky grey ash coated the snowy pavements. The central area around Independence Square was still occupied by the protesters who were firmly entrenched. But they were understandably shaken. A massive undercurrent of paranoia and defiance had consumed them. They were wounded but not defeated.

I walked across the bloodstained, cobblestoned streets of the square at dusk on a night when the temperature hovered a few degrees above zero. I saw nationalists wearing balaclavas and carrying baseball bats and slim planks of wood. These were the men of the night watch. There were no signs of government forces or police, just large barricades and neat lines of Molotov cocktails behind the protesters. It was an eerie atmosphere. I was struck by how the people stuck together. Strangers had fought and died alongside each other, and now they protected one another.

The hotel where I was filing my live reports to the news-room back in Australia had been turned into a makeshift hospital. Wounded fighters recovered in the foyer while doctors and nurses arrived to treat their wounds.

Tensions rose sharply during the grey daylight hours. Out of curiosity, I asked one protester walking near a government building in Independence Square what he kept in his backpack. He opened it for me. Inside was a Molotov cocktail, along with a small bottle of vodka. He proudly told me, 'You cannot be too careful at a time like this.'

On the topic of pride, the protesters had no interest in ransacking the city. With no police around, it must have been a temptation for some opportunists. The burnt shells of cars and buses had been used as roadblocks during the street battles to separate protesters from police, but Kiev's beautiful buildings mostly remained untouched – at least from what I could see. In fact, we filmed lines of ultra-nationalists standing side by side, holding shields, their faces covered by scarves. They were standing in front of government buildings and banks to protect them against thieves. One of the self-appointed guards told me, 'Even though this is an unstable time, there are still looters who might try and take advantage. That is not what this is about. We are the new guardians of the city.'

But not everyone had a positive intention. The city, I was told, needed to be cleansed of pro-Russian sentiment. Putin had tried to meddle in the Ukrainians' affairs so word was out to rid the city of anyone who may have been on the Russian president's side. I saw a politician who was sympathetic to the Russian cause get picked up on the street. It was a pack mentality. Dozens of people spat verbal abuse at him and demanded he be lynched as a warning to the others. As he was taken to a nearby building by a few heavy-set men, other people grabbed at him and tore at his clothing. He was pushed and shoved in what I feared might become a swift version of ugly street justice. I don't know what happened to him but I saw the petrified look on his face as he was dragged past me and taken away.

That image contrasted heavily with the public funerals for about a hundred protesters in total who were killed. The death toll increased after 20 February because of severe injuries that later proved fatal. They were called the Heavenly Hundred and included scientists, musicians, engineers, students, painters and journalists. Open-casket funeral processions weaved through the city. The coffins were held aloft on people's shoulders as the bodies of protesters of varying ages were taken to their graves. Family members dressed in black wept as they walked behind a slow and deeply moving parade. Candles and floral tributes were laid in public places around the city to mourn the dead.

The elephant in the room loomed large. As long as Viktor Yanukovych remained president, nothing would change. The US government upped the ante and slugged him with sanctions, including asset freezes and travel bans, but he was too rich and powerful to care. While many people in Ukraine struggled to get by, Yanukovych was worth billions of dollars and lived like a king. He owned several luxurious mansions and refused to give up his seat on the throne. On 21 February 2014, when the protests had escalated, he had fled the country and, the next day, an interim parliament voted to remove him from power. At the same time, his sprawling estate on the outskirts of Kiev was overrun by Ukrainians who stood amazed at the bastion of wealth arrayed before them. Amongst the gold-plated antiques and priceless views across stunning man-made lakes, there was even a private zoo. It was almost as if their president was mocking them.

Yanukovych never came back. The revolution was complete and on the night it was declared – 22 February – I stood in the crowd and observed the happy and relieved faces. People laughed again. They held each other, and lovers danced. I had seen similar scenes in Egypt in 2011 when Hosni Mubarak was toppled as leader. It was a chance for a new start. But along with all the tears of joy were tears of sorrow for the protesters who'd lost their lives. They were remembered as speaker after speaker stepped on stage and thanked them for their sacrifice. They had become martyrs. Freedom can be taken for granted, and now that it was back again, the first thing Ukraine did was agree to join the European Union.

Trouble was brewing in the country's mostly Russian-speaking east, however, where Yanukovych was born. One of their own had been ousted from office and the people in the region weren't happy.

Over in Moscow, Putin believed his mate Yanukovych had been illegitimately forced from office. Russia described it as a coup and suggested the West had played a strong intervening hand. An arrest warrant was issued for Yanukovych in Ukraine, but he sought and found asylum in Russia. The Russian parliament voted to use force in Ukraine to protect Russian interests. Incursion. Invasion. Call it what you like.

First up was the Crimean Peninsula, which Russia annexed from Ukraine on 18 March 2014. Next was the much larger region of Donetsk Oblast. Not such a simple land grab. But if Putin couldn't have all of Ukraine, he would at least take some of it. Donetsk was where the war erupted and would rumble on for most of 2014. It was also where the world would be shocked by a sinister plane crash.

•

In April 2014 I was led through the headquarters of pro-Russian separatists who had taken over the main government building in Donetsk – the second largest city in Ukraine. In the forecourt of the building, sandbags were piled high, forming an enclosed walkway that snaked its way into the building's entrance. Makeshift wire fences guarded that sandbagged walkway, while masked gunmen patrolled the perimeter. It was very well fortified.

I wanted to talk to the men who were leading the fight against the Ukrainian military. It was mid-April, a few months after the massacre in Kiev and a month after Russia's annexation of Crimea. Ukraine was gripped by a full-blown crisis. The region around Donetsk was divided between those who wanted to remain part of Ukraine and those who wanted to be part of an expanded Russia. Ukraine's military was up against pro-Russian militia that were supported by Russian troops, but the talking was done at executive levels. Ukraine and Russia's leadership talked about de-escalation, but the situation had slowly descended into an all-out conflict. Borders were potentially shifting.

There was no mistaking where allegiances lay in the building I was walking into. Russian flags flapped in the breeze and posters from the Soviet era were stuck to the walls. To get to the higher-ranking officials I had to climb seven storeys of stairs past well-fortified metal doors that had been built inside the stairwell, past rooms filled with boxes of weapons and ammunition, and past the gazing eyes of separatists who may have been suspicious of an intruding film crew.

I was led to a room along with Luke, my translator Mansur, and security consultant Tony, where we met three burly men dressed in army fatigues. Their faces were covered with balaclavas. They always were in Ukraine. The men didn't seem like they were in a mood to muck around. There had been a number of recent attacks, in Slovyansk to the north and Mariupol to our south. The air was stale and the mood was tense.

A map was sprawled out on a desk, and the men pointed out positions where they knew Ukrainian soldiers were based. They indicated where units or battalions were situated. They also showed us where they had recently made successful gains but of course denied they'd made any losses. I was certain that I was being given a fair dose of propaganda but it did seem likely that the building we were in was where many attacks were planned.

One of the men asked me, 'Why is it that what happened in Kiev was called a revolution, while what we are doing is branded as terrorism?' In no uncertain terms he continued, 'We don't want to belong to Ukraine.'

The separatists were strategically smart. Not only did they seize police stations and weapons facilities early in the conflict, but they also captured TV and radio studios so they could broadcast their messages and propaganda. Several days later, Luke and I followed hundreds of people as they simply walked up to one of the main television stations, broke down the gates and flooded into the building. The guards who had been 'protecting' it could only stand and watch.

A few days before, I had reported from Slovyansk. It was a small town about two hours drive north of Donetsk and it seemed fairly insignificant. But it had become a hotbed of violence and a scene of daily attacks because pro-Russian militias had infiltrated it and made it something of a regional base. We drove around its well-protected and well-armed neighbourhoods. I saw groups of soldiers being trained, while seized Ukrainian military tanks roamed the streets and ammunition, including rockets, was hidden behind walls of sandbags. The town had prepared itself for war. The morning we arrived in the city of Donetsk a Ukrainian military helicopter had been shot out of the sky, although it was impossible to filter the truth from the huge lumps of propaganda that were being fed to us from both directions.

What I did notice was the presence of so-called 'little green men'. These were soldiers in green military clothing without any apparent insignia who were first spotted in Crimea before it was annexed. It was strongly suspected they were Russian agents taking orders from the Russian government. I met one of them in Slovyansk. A stocky fellow, aged in his fifties, who sported a white beard. He didn't give a name or a rank but he seemed to be in control of the city.

I asked him about the accusations. 'Are there any Russian soldiers in Slovyansk?'

'*Niet*,' he calmly replied. Through a translator, he told me, 'Americans are just amateurs who want to make fiction appear real. To them all Russians look alike.'

I didn't believe him at all. But we were on his turf so I wasn't prepared to challenge him. He didn't seem troubled by our presence either, which was good because Slovyansk had developed a nasty reputation – journalists had been kidnapped there and tortured.

A month later on a return trip, we had a gun pointed at us in Slovyansk. Our van was pulled over by separatists at a sandbagged roadblock. We had placed a small GoPro camera on the dashboard and it filmed a soldier aiming his weapon at us as we were ordered out of the vehicle. The barrel of the rifle followed our movements as we were herded into a little group off the side of the road. We stood nervously and watched as the soldiers rummaged through our gear and took some of our protective equipment. They wanted all of it, and regularly spoke to superiors on their radios about what to do next. The only other time something like this had happened was in Rio de Janeiro in 2009 when I was sent to cover the wars between police and drug runners. I had ventured too far inside a favela where a man pulled me up and in a Portuguese–English accent said, 'Sir, I suggest you turn back.' 'Why?' I asked. He said, 'Because there is a gun pointed at you from a home across the street. This place is not for you or your camera.' I duly obliged.

As we often did in the Middle East, we played up the Australian angle because (usually) people don't have much beef with Australians. The British and American reporters had it much worse. But regardless of nationality, being ordered out of a vehicle and having equipment searched was always a nerve-racking experience. I was never sure what people would do. I certainly knew what these men were capable of, and because many of the soldiers were drunk, accidents could happen in a tense environment, especially from people who had itchy trigger fingers. Usually, soldiers would surround us and try to intimidate us by letting us know what they could do. Fortunately, on this occasion, they detained us for only a short while before they told us to get back in the van and drive back to our hotel in Donetsk.

I saw a lot of the Ukrainian countryside because we spent hours every day driving from town to town, cramped in the back of a van, checking areas that had been attacked. *This is what they are fighting for*, I would think. Land. Land that didn't really have a great deal on it. You could drive hundreds of kilometres and not see anything other than dry barren fields. We'd sometimes drive to the Russian border, past the open fields where Malaysian Airlines Flight 17 would be shot out of the sky later that year. We would often see Ukrainian and, we suspected, Russian military units hiding their tanks in bushland. But that was it.

During our time travelling around the countryside, I often thought of how Ukraine had looked only two years before, during the European football championships of 2012. Millions of dollars had been poured into the country to modernise its roads, its transport systems, its airports and its stadiums. Thousands of football fans from all over the world came to Ukraine's cities to watch some of the greatest footballers in history compete. It seemed then like a country that had moved so far since the collapse of the Soviet Union.

Just eighteen months later, the nation was in worse shape than it had been in decades. Shahktar Donetsk Football Club, a powerhouse in the region, had had to relocate because their stadium had been targeted by several rocket attacks. The brand-new airport, built especially for the Euro 2012 tournament and which we'd often flown in and out of, was completely destroyed by the war. Then of course there were the people. It's always the people who feel it the most. Many had had their homes and even their lives taken away. The death toll was mounting. For what cause? To what end?

●

Two years before the Ukrainian war, I had been in Moscow. The weather was bitterly cold. Well below zero. When it wasn't snowing, a strong wind chill blasted my face with the kind of cold that burns. The cold also came up through the icy cobblestoned ground and froze my feet, despite the thick boots I wore. When your feet are cold, your whole body is cold. It was 4 March 2012, and I was standing among a huge crowd of people who had gathered near Red Square outside the walls of the Kremlin. Body warmth meant nothing; we all shivered together. Red cheeks and red noses on Red Square. Some of the people waved flags and swilled vodka from bottles they carried in the pockets of their puffy jackets.

The focal point up on stage a few metres in front of me was a figure of history – the last tsar of Russia, Vladimir Putin. He seemed shorter than I imagined him to be, but any perceived lack of height was quickly replaced by the serious presence he carried. Putin was president again. He had just declared victory in his latest controversial election campaign, having served two terms as prime minister, which followed his first two terms as president. Russian law states a president can only serve two consecutive six-year terms.

'We have won in an open and fair struggle,' Putin told his supporters as tears rolled down his cheeks. A rare show of emotion from the former KGB strongman. Or maybe it was just the cold.

'This was more than just a presidential election. This was a very important test for us – a test for the political maturity of our people and independence,' he told thousands of listeners. I doubted everyone there supported him, and I knew that many people didn't believe a word he said.

Putin had his critics within Russia's vast borders, of that you can be sure. During the election campaign, there had been more public opposition than ever before, and the word was that Putin was rattled. Usually people were too afraid to oppose him, or any other Russian regime for that matter, out of fear they would be sent away to one of the nation's brutal jails or gulags, or rubbed out completely – often in mysterious circumstances. It had happened. The 2012 election drew extra international attention thanks to the female punk rock band Pussy Riot, whose members wore coloured balaclavas and performed anti-regime songs in front of public places. Two of its leading members were jailed. The band was popular because they sang about injustices, and pointed to a corrupt government led by a corrupt president. It was a feeling shared by a growing portion of the community. There were protests and even riots when the members were sent to prison. I went to a couple of protests and could only wonder how many government spies were in the crowd. We were told more than once to be very careful. Russia, it was claimed, was the fourth most dangerous country in the world for journalists to work. Between the years 2000 and 2009, twenty journalists were killed and only one person was convicted in relation to any of those deaths.

Perhaps the Russian people were also energised by the events of the so-called 2011 Arab Spring in the Middle East, where brutal dictators were ousted from power. They might have thought, 'Hey, if Egypt and Libya can do it, why can't we?' But that mindset would not work in Russia for one very good reason – the number of people who liked Putin far outnumbered those who didn't. Putin wielded significant power, influence and financial muscle. Even though many claimed the 2012 election had a certain stench to it, the official result had Putin claiming more than 60 per cent of the overall vote. In other words, he won in a landslide.

Putin's influence didn't stop at Russia's borders. It crossed into Europe and Central Asia. It was felt in neighbouring Belarus, in Georgia, and especially in Ukraine or 'Little Russia'.

Two years later, as war rumbled on in Ukraine's east, I would think of Putin's power whenever I spoke to separatists. The power that he presented on that stage in Moscow: it was as if I heard it in the words of fighters, and saw it on the faces of innocent citizens and on the many dead bodies I saw lying on the streets. Ordinary people who had become statistics. Their deaths would not be avenged, and no one would be held accountable. All that was left was for a mother or a wife or a child to grieve. Even with the disgraceful attack on MH17, in which 298 civilians were killed, including thirty-three Australians, what started as thunderous rhetoric from world leaders who promised action all but faded away. As Putin critic Garry Kasparov wrote in his book *Winter is Coming*: 'As long as Putin is in office we'll never know who gave the order, but there is no doubt that he is directly responsible for creating the conditions in which these outrages occur with such terrible frequency.'

Russia's involvement in Ukraine was always denied at an official level, but it was obvious on the streets. Any fool could see the Russian tanks and Russian weapons that were supplied to fighters.

'Whose side are you on?' the separatists would ask whenever I spoke to them or filmed stories inside their bases or hideouts. Intimidation was rife, as was propaganda.

I felt sorry for those Ukrainians who weren't pro-Russian in areas like Donetsk. They wanted to be part of the new Ukraine that had been established in Kiev at the start of 2014. But the east of Ukraine felt so far from the west, where Kiev was, and towards the end of 2014 any hope for freedom, or just a lull in the war, was no more than a dream. Pro-Ukrainian residents were too afraid to speak up. They were trapped in a war zone. Just surviving was the best they could hope for. Families had to live in bomb shelters or underground hideouts, because it was too unsafe to be anywhere else. Many weren't so lucky.

It was mob rule in the east and Ukraine was being carved up by the various militias and fighting forces. It reminded me of the situation in Libya after the 2011 revolution. There was no law or order, and many weapons facilities inside police stations had been raided, so guns were prevalent. No one could be trusted.

In May 2014 I saw how bad things in Ukraine had become when I was filming a story on a military base in

Mariupol that was being raided by separatists. Hours earlier, sleeping Ukrainian soldiers had been woken by an invading army of Russian separatists. The soldiers were surprisingly unprepared for an attack and hundreds of them were chased off the base, leaving their belongings and weapons behind. When I was at the military base, there wasn't a single member of the military there. I watched mostly young masked men walk in from the streets, enter the base, sift through the soldiers' halls, and gladly scoop up whatever they could find. Guns, shields, personal belongings, food, water. It was a free-for-all, and no one could be punished for it. I tried to talk to some of the masked men but they scurried away.

Towards the end of 2014, I narrowly missed a heavy firefight in the port city of Mariupol.

My crew and I arrived to find the separatists' local headquarters up in flames and we were suddenly surrounded by a large group of armed men. They were red-hot with rage and fuelled by alcohol. The old government building that they had used as a local command post, where we had filmed several stories before, had been destroyed by Ukrainian military tanks that had swiftly and unexpectedly moved in and shot it down. The building was smouldering and the roads were littered with shell casings from the live rounds of ammunition. The aggressive separatists dragged us around the battle scene and showed us examples of what they claimed was the brutality of the Ukrainian military. 'They fired on us. They fired on us, unprovoked,' they shouted.

Around the corner, the scene was much worse. A police station was well alight. Large columns of smoke rose into the sky. A fire truck was trying to put out the remaining fires, which threatened to spread towards other buildings. Again, shell casings covered the bitumen pavement. I saw the body of a middle-aged police officer lying on the street. He was still wearing his uniform. His mouth was slightly open, while the narrow slits of his lifeless eyes gazed skywards. Another dead body was further up the street. This man was plain-clothed. At least someone had covered his face with a sheet. Two more men lost to a pointless war. I stared at them for a short while, and wondered who they'd left behind. Who would mourn them that night? Then gunfire cracked in the distance, and I remembered where I was. At war, where this kind of sight was common.

•

Now in 2016 there is an uneasy peace in eastern Ukraine. Russia's army has retreated and the world's media has moved on. A ceasefire has been in place for almost a year. According to the United Nations about eight thousand people lost their lives in the conflict. It's a death toll that began to climb on a cold night in Kiev towards the end of 2013.

I sometimes wonder what would have happened if those first protesters at Kiev's Independence Square were told, 'You will win this battle, the president will be forced from office and into exile. But it will come at a cost. The country will be plunged into war and thousands of your countrymen and women will be killed.'

Would they still have thought it was worth it? Or would they have packed up and gone home and continued to live in an oppressed state? I guess the same question could be asked of the protesters in Egypt and Libya, and Syria. Some people might claim that no cause is worth dying for. Others might tell me that the people didn't die for nothing, they fought for what they believed in.

Chapter 7

THE NIGHT I MET A TERRORIST

THE LONDON RIOTS ────────────

I wasn't to know he was a terrorist. No one could have known. Perhaps not even he knew at the time. But there were some troubling signs.

It was London, 6 August 2011, and the city was about to explode in seething and contagious fits of rage.

Just before midnight, I made the short dash across town from my apartment in Fulham, west of the capital, to the northern suburb of Tottenham, where the dynamite was sparked. As soon as I got out of the taxi, I could see huge bright flames stretching high into the night sky. Double-decker buses were alight, police cars had been destroyed, and buildings were burning down. It was absolute chaos. Whole streets were on fire with the silhouettes of protesters and police standing in the foreground. It was the kind of scene I was familiar with from my time in Africa and the Middle

East – after all, it was the year of the Arab uprisings – but it was the last thing I expected to see in England. The anarchists had taken control.

I met up with my cameraman, James Gillings. Riot police pushed us back with other journalists and spectators as armed officers tried to wrest back control. They held their shields up to protect their faces, and tried to hold defensive lines while rioters hurled whatever missiles they could find – rocks, bricks, even long pieces of timber. I could hear the sounds of bottles smashing and glass breaking while police helicopters flew overhead. The rioters seemed to be mostly young and the longer it went on, the more emboldened they became.

The riots were in response to the death of Mark Duggan, a young local man, who had been killed by police on 4 August 2011. The black community where he lived rose up and protested against the police, accusing them of a racially motivated attack. Police were later cleared of any wrongdoing as Duggan was alleged to have fired his weapon at officers and been involved in criminal gangs.

The fallout had started as a protest, but quickly escalated into the full-blown outbreak of violence I was now witnessing.

I was keen to find someone to interview as I wanted to provide viewers back in Australia with some thoughts about what was unravelling, and also some commentary on race relations between police and the black community. A few people around us had become quite heated and so I turned the microphone their way. That's how I found Abdel-Majed Abdel Bary, or rather how he found me.

Abdel Bary was a young English man of Egyptian heritage who was outraged at what he claimed was police brutality. Dressed in ordinary clothing, he had long frizzy hair that was tied back underneath a flat-brimmed baseball cap, and he had a bit of facial fluff on his lip and chin. Speaking with a thick East London accent, he launched into an angry tirade. 'I was there for three hours, yeah. There's a bus on fire. It started off as a little fire.'

He became more animated as he continued. People started to cheer him on and so he gesticulated like a rap musician at every beat of the lines he was spinning to me. 'The police are protecting the police, they're not protecting the people. The policeman said it out of his own words when I asked him, "Why are you here?" He said, "I'm here to protect the police!"'

I think I only asked one question but Abdel Bary's response went on for several minutes. I didn't interrupt him.

The interview wasn't anything special at the time. Abdel Bary had a point to make and was obviously passionate, but it wasn't so remarkable that it stood out beyond any of the other conversations I had that night. It was just one man's rant during a violent outbreak. He may have just been hamming it up for the camera.

The interview only became significant three years later when the Syrian war was more than three years old and Abdel Bary was named as a key suspect in the hunt for the so-called Jihadi John – the masked man with the British accent who had decapitated several Western journalists and aid workers who were kidnapped by militants in Syria. The beheadings were used in Islamic State's ultra-violent propaganda videos that shocked and sickened the world. *The Times* of London broke the story about an investigation into the link between Abdel Bary and Jihadi John, which was picked up by media outlets across Europe, America and Australia. His face was all over the British tabloids. I was out of the country on another assignment at the time but James remembered him from the riots so he dug up our old interview, which we then aired in our next story on Channel Nine's evening news. Did we interview the man who would later become the world's most wanted terrorist?

Our old interview from the London riots was replayed on British television by news networks, and quotes from Abdel Bary were reprinted in British, American and Australian newspapers. It was something of an accidental scoop for our little foreign bureau.

Abdel Bary was a slim, light-skinned rapper who became radicalised some time after the London riots. Some of his lyrics document his path to extremism.

'I'm trying to change my ways but there's blood on my hands and I can't change my ways until there's funds in the bank,' he rapped.

'I can't differentiate the angels from the demons, my heart's disintegrating. I ain't got normal feelings,' he rhymed in another tune.

Abdel Bary may have been destined for extremism because his father Adel Abdel Bary was an Egyptian militant with a serious history of extremist action. He was a close associate of Osama bin Laden and Ayman al-Zawahiri, who replaced bin Laden as leader of al-Qaeda. Adel Abdel Bary was himself a member of al-Qaeda and was said to have been imprisoned and tortured in Egypt following the death of President Anwar Sadat in 1981.

After he and his family were given political asylum in Britain in 1993, he was extradited to the United States in 2012 where he confessed to his involvement in the bombings of two US embassies in East Africa in 1998 that had resulted in the deaths of 224 people. In 2015, he was sentenced to twenty-five years in jail. Back in London, his 24-year-old son may have held a sizeable grudge.

Some time after the London riots, and about the same time his father was facing court in the US, Abdel-Majed Abdel Bary was radicalised by Muslim groups in England. He tossed aside his music career and followed his father's footsteps into the desert. But al-Qaeda didn't interest him. A much more sinister, more violent terror group was his calling – the Islamic State.

Proof of Abdel Bary's involvement with IS was found in a sickening photograph that was posted online in early August 2014. The photograph was tweeted from an account that apparently belonged to him. It was allegedly taken inside the IS headquarters of Raqqa in northern Syria and showed the man I'd met three years prior holding a decapitated head. It was accompanied by a caption that read 'Chillin' with my homie or what's left of him'.

When I saw the photograph, I couldn't quite believe it. I wouldn't even pretend to know Abdel Bary as we'd only had a short exchange during a brief encounter. But looking at the photograph was like looking at a ghost. When we lined it up with our old interview, I was temporarily lost for words. It was definitely him. The rapper had become a killer in the world's most feared terrorist organisation. But was he the most wanted man? Was he Jihadi John?

An investigation by the British newspaper *The Mail on Sunday* claimed Bary was a member of 'the Beatles' – a nickname given by Western captives to a group of four British-born IS members who guarded, tortured, and beheaded foreign hostages in Syria. But which one of them was John?

Following analysis of video and voice patterns, American and British authorities named Mohammad Emwazi as Jihadi John. Born in Kuwait, raised and educated in the UK, Emwazi was radicalised and had trodden the well-worn path to Syria before he was killed by a US and British drone attack in 2015.

Abdel Bary might not have been Jihadi John, but it seemed certain he was fighting with IS, perhaps even as one of the other 'Beatles'.

It's near impossible to confirm but there were reports he had left the terror group, and as of July 2015 was on the run somewhere in Turkey. If that's true, he's got a major problem because he's wanted by two sets of people: British security services and ISIS executioners who don't take too kindly to anyone who deserts their ranks.

•

After Tottenham burned on night one of the 2011 London riots, the flames quickly spread to other parts of the country, and really took hold on night two in suburbs south of London, including Croydon and Peckham. James and I drove through the eerie streets in the early evening and were amazed at what we saw in such a developed city. Hundreds of homes were damaged and the burnt shells of cars sat on the streets while sirens blared in the distance. Brixton, Hackney, Ealing, Barking, Battersea and Lewisham were all caught in the chaos. These suburbs weren't that far from where we lived in Fulham and it seemed surreal that such chaos could be so close to home.

People had to jump out of burning buildings in the confusion and desperation. An old furniture store had been set on fire and the large fingers of flames stretched high into the night sky. There wasn't a police vehicle in sight as rioters seized control, spreading their messages and rallying cries on social media, which was difficult for authorities to prevent.

What began as a race riot or political protest turned into class warfare as disadvantaged youths from the poorer suburbs joined in on the law-breaking and vandalism. We drove through the main streets of Peckham and saw looters break into stores and take what they wanted. I stood in a dark street as dozens of people broke through the security doors of a jewellery store and grabbed what they pleased. No one was worried about being caught. I was talking on my phone during an interview with the *Today* show when a young looter barged up to me and brazenly asked if I was a cop. On the high street of Croydon, thousands of people were smashing windows and climbing into shops to steal shoes and clothes. They ripped TVs off the walls and took whatever electrical goods they could carry. Some people even used shopping trolleys to roll their loot home.

Most of the looters were dumb though. Some posed for photographs with their stolen merchandise and many didn't cover their faces as they pilfered from shops in front of news cameras. Later, this would work to the advantage of investigators who arrested more than 2000 offenders. It was terrific police work as they trawled through the internet and used the rioters' own videos and photographs against them.

Unrest seemed to be a worldwide theme in 2011, and now London was caught up in it. Dictators had tumbled, and now it seemed that David Cameron, a democratically elected leader of the Western world who had only just been voted in, might fall on his sword. It might seem far-fetched and unlikely, but following Duggan's death it was potentially a prelude to his premature exit.

The images of looters in London suburbs became headline news around the world and there was pressure for the government to send the army out to restore control, but

Home Secretary Theresa May kiboshed that idea because it wouldn't be a good look and might set a dangerous precedent. But something needed to be done. A 68-year-old man was killed on the streets of Ealing as he tried to stamp out a rubbish bin fire that had been lit by rioters who then attacked the old man for getting involved. Dozens of other people were either attacked or mugged.

Then it got even worse. On nights three and four, upheaval spread north beyond the capital and into the nation's other large cities, including Manchester and Birmingham. The London riots became the England riots. Shop windows were broken and businesses destroyed as gangs of youths and young adults owned the night.

Britain is no stranger to riots. They're actually quite regular. I'd even covered a large and violent student protest with Jimmy earlier in 2011. We had been pushed around by wild protesters and police on horseback but riot police had brought it under control within a few hours. But this time things were different and many people were claiming the riots were worse than the violent and deadly Brixton riots of the 1980s.

A much larger police presence was eventually deployed and, after four dangerous nights, police gained the upper hand and restored peace to the country. Clean-up campaigns began as citizens pitched in and helped tidy up the streets. Some, including the London mayor Boris Johnson, whom I had interviewed from time to time, grabbed their own brooms and dug in. Communities that had been divided and living in fear were now working together and turning a wrong into a right.

•

Two years after the London riots in 2011, I was back reporting in London on another violent event, but this time it was an act of terrorism.

Britain is also no stranger to terrorism. Far from it. There had been dozens of attacks since the 1960s, mostly to do with 'The Troubles' during England's long war with the IRA. In 2011 I spent time in the Irish city of Cork with former IRA leader Martin McGuinness during his failed election campaign to become President of Ireland. Whenever I steered the conversation towards IRA involvement in terrorist attacks or the war itself, he directed the interview back to the future. Later, he met the Queen in Belfast in a highly publicised PR move for reconciliation. As James and I filmed the many political murals of Northern Ireland, and the walls that separated the unionists and the nationalists, we sensed there was still an undercurrent of tension between the two sides. War does that. It's hard to forgive and it's harder to forget. But the face of terror in the United Kingdom changed over the years.

The bombings of 7 July 2005 signalled the arrival of Islamic extremism in the United Kingdom, and in the following years the country became a breeding ground for terrorists who emerged from the same suburbs as the rioters of 2011. Some British citizens, like some Australians, have fought with IS in Syria and Iraq and then returned home. Governments are understandably concerned about returning fighters.

Michael Adebolajo and Michael Adebowale were not returned fighters but homegrown terrorists. They were both British of Nigerian descent, both Christians who converted to Islam, and both radicalised with links to al-Qaeda. The victim they chose for their random attack was British army soldier Fusilier Lee Rigby.

It was a clear afternoon. Rigby was off duty and walking to the Woolwich Army Barracks in south-east London when a small car sped towards him at about sixty kilometres an hour as he crossed the road. The car struck Rigby and ran him over. His attackers then climbed out of the blue Vauxhall Tigra and approached Rigby's wounded body. They pulled out knives and a cleaver and stabbed him several times before they tried to behead him in front of stunned and frightened onlookers. One of the witnesses filmed the attackers on a mobile phone, which attracted the attention of killer Michael Adebolajo who gesticulated to the camera during a heated ninety-second rant with two murder weapons and blood-soaked hands:

The only reason we have killed this man today is because Muslims are dying daily by British soldiers and this British soldier is one. It is an eye for an eye and a tooth for a tooth. By Allah, we swear by the almighty Allah we will never stop fighting you until you leave us alone.

On and on he went, railing about perceived injustices. There was no attempt by the two Michaels to hide themselves or run away. There would be no siege or police chase. Police arrived within minutes and arrested the pair. The scene was my reporting base for the next few days and, while it was far from being a big terror attack, the story was powerful because it was such a rare act of savage brutality and anyone could have been the victim.

Rigby's death triggered a massive outpouring of grief as walls of flowers and heartfelt messages were left at the army barracks where the fusilier was killed. The British attackers were convicted of murder. Adebolajo was sentenced to life imprisonment while Adebowale got forty-five years. Both of the men had been on Britain's terror watchlist because Adebolajo had been caught in Kenya years earlier while trying to train with the Somali al-Qaeda affiliate al-Shabab. The British government came in for plenty of stick but there are thousands of people on the various watchlists around the world so it's difficult to track all of them at the same time. The holes in the system have been exploited many times over. As IS rose to power it actively encouraged its supporters and followers to perform these random attacks on the street. Indeed, some potential attackers have even been caught in Australia before the act of terror was carried out.

The attacks and riots point to a wider problem in society. As former British Prime Minister Tony Blair said after Rigby's death, there's no problem with Islam itself because most Muslims are peace-loving people. But there is a problem within Islam and that can lead to extremism. Youths and vulnerable kids are brainwashed by preachers of hate in places of lower socioeconomic standing. It happened to Abdel Bary. It happened to Michael Adebolajo. It happened to Michael Adebowale. It happened to the terrorists of France in 2015, and in Belgium a year later, and it's going to happen again.

Chapter 8

HOPE AND DESPAIR IN A LOST CITY

THE HAITI EARTHQUAKE ————————————

Some moments in life don't leave much of an imprint on your soul, they tend to fade away as fast as they appear. Other moments attach themselves to you, like a barnacle on a rock, and become part of who you are. Months, years, decades pass. Good times and bad. Yet throughout it all, those moments are still hanging onto you, affecting every decision you make. Haiti was one such barnacle for me.

•

It was 12 January 2010 and I'd just arrived at California's Mammoth Mountain for a few days of snowboarding with friends when the news broke about a large earthquake in Haiti. The true extent of the damage wouldn't be known for several hours but the pictures looked awfully bad. Veteran Channel Nine correspondent Rob Penfold and cameraman Rich Moran had already been dispatched to the region and I was told that backup might be needed. Sure enough, on the following morning, confirmation came from my editors in Sydney that a second journalist was required to cover the story, so I jumped straight back in my car and drove seven hours to Los Angeles Airport. I was joined by cameraman Brian Russell who had flown in from the Gold Coast. My seven-hour drive to LAX was followed by a flight to the Dominican Republic because the airport in Haiti was too badly damaged to fly into.

Brian and I arrived in a hot and chaotic Santo Domingo, the capital of the Dominican Republic. Haiti and the Dominican Republic are both located on the large island of Hispaniola. Aid workers, journalists, and government representatives had all flown in at the same time and were now scrambling to find transport to Haiti. Brian and I were hooked up with a driver and a translator who drove us east to Haiti and the earthquake zone. It took most of the following day to get there as we travelled along the scenic skinny Caribbean streets until we arrived in Haiti's capital, Port-au-Prince, at dusk. The scene was disturbing and confronting. The powerful 7.0 quake shook the small Caribbean nation at about five o'clock in the afternoon when most of the kids were home from school. The tremor lasted for about forty seconds, but many of the victims said their bones were still shaking hours later. More than a million

Haitians were too afraid of aftershocks to return home, so they slept under sheets and in tents out on the streets. Chances were they didn't have a home to return to anyway.

Rob and Rich had found one of the few hotels that were still standing, which was also occupied by journalists from other world networks, including the big stars of American TV such as Anderson Cooper from CNN.

By morning I quickly learned how utterly tragic the situation was. Many Haitians said they thought the moment the earthquake hit was the end of the world, which wasn't an overstatement because the city looked apocalyptic. Buildings, shops, and businesses had crumbled to the ground and debris was scattered across the dirt streets. It wasn't just a few buildings either; there were whole suburbs of flattened concrete. Even the Presidential Palace, the biggest and surely sturdiest building in the country, had collapsed. But the sight of damaged homes and buildings was overpowered by the sickly stench of death. I walked through the city ruins and saw bloated bodies lying on the ground. The sight of arms and legs sticking out of debris was common. The dead skin had a wax-like sheen, while other bodies were coated in thick layers of dirt and dust.

One rescue worker wearing a face mask dragged a corpse out from underneath the rubble and left it on the street before returning to the collapsed building to search for more bodies. Some of the dead were left alone, while others were stacked into piles. Corpses were collected on wheelbarrows and shopping trolleys while others were thrown onto pyres made from burning tyres. The car park of the Port-au-Prince Hospital became an outdoor morgue as dead bodies were laid out on the open ground, left for the flies and the hungry chickens. It's not so hard to figure out how disease became so rampant.

Sometimes signs could be seen at the front of a shattered home: '2 BODIES HERE. HELP!' But help was slow to arrive. The airport was so badly damaged that aid and rescue teams were diverted to the Dominican Republic and had to make the slow drive in just as we had. There were so many bodies that, within a few short days, garbage trucks were driven around the city to collect the dead and the corpses were simply tossed inside. I didn't even need to see the truck or hear it to know it was close; I could smell it as it worked its way around the city picking up people's remains.

The death toll was so high that individual funerals would have taken too long to organise and carry out, so bodies were driven to the outskirts of the capital and dropped into mass graves. Many people who survived the quake didn't even have the chance to say goodbye to family or friends. If anyone was missing it was assumed they had been taken away and disposed of and their family would never know where their loved one's final resting place was. The scene was so horrific and so desperate that I don't think the authorities had any other choice but to act quickly to bury the bodies.

I filmed a piece at the Port-au-Prince federal prison where up to 3000 inmates were kept before the quake. Most of them were in jail for murder, rape and other violent crimes.

But when the city started to sway they were just as frightened as everyone else. Hundreds of them broke through the bars or windows and fled into the streets; those who stayed behind were crushed and killed. It made Port-au-Prince even more intense, knowing the nation's most violent criminals were back on the outside.

While the killers were out on the streets, so were the looters. Haiti is dirt poor. It is a third-world country, which has suffered from chronic poverty and with an unstable government since its French colonial era. A healthy life expectancy for a Haitian is just sixty years, an average that has been brought down by malnutrition and diseases such as HIV/AIDS. There wasn't much work around and those who could hold on to a job earned about 650 dollars a year. So when law and order vanished, hundreds of mostly young men seized the chance to steal whatever they could. Police tried to make arrests but it was a futile task. Where would the offenders be taken? Police stations, prisons, and army barracks had all been destroyed. That's why thieves were shot dead on the spot. Chaos reigned. Frustration ruled. Buildings and churches were set on fire, which fitted in perfectly with the apocalyptic atmosphere. Personally, I didn't feel threatened. Although when one of our translators was seen one evening carrying a handgun, he needed to be let go. We weren't sure why he had it. For protection? Or just to feel like a strong man? Either way, we couldn't work with that around.

The death toll quickly spiralled beyond belief and the situation on the ground was dire. Fresh food and drinking water had become scarce but what was more concerning was that medical supplies were rapidly depleted. Hospitals and infrastructure hadn't been in great shape to begin with due to the country's poverty. Thousands of people had sustained crippling injuries that in some cases had turned gangrenous, which meant limbs had to be surgically removed or else infection would spread. If that wasn't bad enough there wasn't much in the way of anaesthetics. It was also apparent that proper surgical tools weren't available to the volunteer doctors so saws and plastic scissors were used during some operations.

Life was so dramatically altered here, even for those who escaped serious injury. Tent cities emerged in open fields because families felt safest away from buildings. Sleeping under a sheet was not going to kill anyone. But the safest places could sometimes become the most dangerous as tempers boiled over and gangs tried to take the limited stocks of food and water. Before the earthquake the country didn't have much in the way of clean drinking water, so after the quake there was even more demand for food and water.

Hillary Clinton, who was a year into her position as US Secretary of State, was the first Western diplomat to arrive in Haiti.

'We will work with your government, under the direction of President Rene Preval, to assist in any way we can,' she told reporters.

Her husband, Bill, had done plenty of work in Haiti through his foundation, and as an expression of unity he stood at the White House with President Obama and former President George W. Bush to show support for the grief-stricken nation.

'It is still one of the most remarkable, unique places I have ever been, and they can escape their history and build a better future,' Clinton said.

Food, water, and much-needed medical supplies slowly found their way into aid distribution points and makeshift hospitals, but that was just for Port-au-Prince. The outside areas had been hit too but they would have to wait even longer for aid.

Five days after the quake, I drove with Brian out to a place called Leogane, the location of the earthquake's epicentre. Huge cavities had split roads into pieces and fields of earth had been carved open. I don't think I saw a single home or structure in one piece. But Leogane had one thing in its favour – a smaller population. It didn't have the built-up neighbourhoods that the capital city had so the death toll was considerably lower. But there were a lot of badly injured survivors.

I sat next to a woman who was eight months pregnant and was lying on the hard ground with infected wounds. Her friend, who also had a badly injured face, was doing her best to fan air onto the woman's sweaty face. I found one young man who summed it all up for me.

'On their faces you can only see misery. They have lost everything they have.'

I stood on top of Leogane's crumpled ruins. There wasn't a rescue team in sight. Port-au-Prince had drained all the resources. People pleaded for help, and had written signs in English appealing to foreign media and aid workers.

When the young man told me that the people of Leogane had lost everything they had, I knew he wasn't talking about material things because there wasn't a great deal of that around. People out there lived on even less than the people of Port-au-Prince. Most of them were on about a dollar a day. All they had were flimsy shanties and it didn't take much for them to fall. The man was talking about the human cost – the dead friends and dead family members who were heaped in piles on the side of the road for pick-up. I assumed they would be there for a while because the roads leading into the town were in terrible condition and food and medicine would be the first priorities. Life in Haiti was tough before the quake. It had just become a whole lot tougher.

•

It was just after six o'clock in the morning on 21 January 2010. I hadn't had much rest so I was passed out in a deep sleep. Brian and I were sharing a room on the second floor of the hotel at Port-au-Prince. Then we were jolted awake by a real-life alarm clock. The walls, the ceiling, and the beds were violently shaking. 'This is it!' Brian yelled. 'Get out!' Was I still asleep? Was it a nightmare? It felt like the room was in the grip of a Godzilla-type giant who was clutching the hotel and shaking it. It took me a few seconds to realise that it was an aftershock and a bloody big one – the strongest aftershock since the original quake nine days earlier.

I rolled off the bed and onto the floor, but when I tried to get up the balls of my feet couldn't grip the ground so I slid out and cracked my knee against the floor. It wasn't a nightmare. It was definitely real because I felt the pain shoot through my body and my heart was pounding hard. Twenty seconds of a 6.1 tremor passed before I was able to get on to my feet and scurry to the door.

Then the aftershock stopped.

The earth was still again.

I looked around and saw Brian standing at the foot of his bed in a pair of red undies. We looked at each other in stunned silence for a short second before I burst into laughter out of nervousness and sheer relief. Then I said, 'Even if I got out the door, where was I going to go?'

It was my first experience of a large quake and I realised that when panic takes over, you lose control of any rational thought. People would have felt like that on 12 January, those who survived anyway.

Aftershocks could finish the job begun by the larger original quake. Already weakened homes or buildings that hadn't fully fallen could be sent crashing to the ground. We learned later that many people screamed during the aftershock and they ran for the open air, and patients at a nearby hospital started to pray. If there had been anybody still living indoors, surely they wouldn't stay there following that aftershock.

The slightest noise could send people running. False alarms were regular. The tiniest bang or an incorrect rumour of an incoming tsunami forced people to run for their lives. And when one person ran it usually meant a stampede. I had seen this often during the desperate search for survivors. Sometimes local teams with no rescue experience would walk into broken buildings and then scurry into the street outside after they heard a noise, thinking it was another aftershock. I don't say that as any sort of criticism, because I would do the same, and did if I was standing too close to the buildings. For over a week we had watched rescue teams walk precariously over broken homes, listening for the slightest sound or cry for help. There had been some amazing stories. I'd never seen a humanitarian mission where so many NGOs and good Samaritans from different parts of the world came to help.

One of the great images came a few days after the quake when New York firefighters picked through the rubble until they heard a noise. A little boy named Kiki was rescued from a deep pit of debris. His house had fallen on top of him but remarkably he was still alive. When Kiki was pulled to the surface he was held aloft and he thrust his arms into the air in victory. A loud cheer came from those who had watched the hours-long operation. Some of those firefighters had battled the aftermath of September 11 and were brought to tears by the rescue. But it wasn't over. Kiki's older sister Sabrina was still trapped inside. Without much time to enjoy the moment, the men and women of the NYFD returned to work and burrowed further into the mire. A short while later the ten-year-old girl was pulled out alive. What a story. It was the sort of stuff that gives people hope. It was why they were working so hard. The death toll was already into the hundreds of thousands but saving one life still made a mark. But even the happiest of stories sometimes have sad endings. Kiki and Sabrina also had a brother who was with them, but he couldn't be saved. He was already dead.

Life or death could also come down to a matter of luck. A few survivors were food shopping in a supermarket before the quake struck. They were buried alive but somehow ended up near the fruit aisle so they had enough sustenance to keep their hearts beating until rescuers found them.

As more time ticked by, the chances of finding survivors dimmed like a light losing power. Hope, like the light, flickered each time a new survivor was found but eventually the brightness ran out. After nearly two weeks, rescue missions gradually became recovery missions.

As the weeks went by and hope for survivors faded to black, urgency returned to the distribution of aid. Outside one of the many large tent cities, bags of rice were kept in storage. But to make sure everyone received equal amounts, the people had to be fenced in, almost as if they were caged animals. Their bodies were pressed up to the steel fence, and their hopeful, hungry eyes peered through. I was on the UN side with Brian where the food was kept. To avoid a stampede, the UN workers allowed two people through at a time and those two people represented different families. I expected bedlam but surprisingly the groups calmly walked through the gate, up to the food distribution point, slung a bag each over their shoulders, then walked back into the fenced-off area and to their families waiting at the tents. If only everything else ran as smoothly.

The hospitals were at breaking point. Makeshift medical centres popped up all over the capital to treat the many wounded people but it wasn't enough. The United States stepped up its relief effort and sent in an armada of ships, including one of the world's biggest – the aircraft carrier USS *Carl Vinson* – as well as the hospital ship USNS *Comfort*. In the month following the quake, the *Comfort*'s navy doctors treated over 1000 Haitians and performed more than 850 surgeries. But eventually, even the hospital ship was full.

Then, when it seemed as though things couldn't get any worse, a silent killer emerged. Months, even years after the world's media had left and moved on to other stories, an outbreak of disease took hold and spread.

When Haiti was under colonial rule the French called the country the 'Pearl of the Antilles' because of its high mountain ranges and natural beauty. But the 7.0 quake and years of abuse transformed much of that beauty into a cesspit of rubbish, pollution, and death, and it was just a matter of time before cholera emerged from that putrid cocktail.

By the end of 2015 the disease had claimed the lives of more than 9000 Haitians, while another 700,000 became sick. It proves that an earthquake doesn't end when the earth stops shaking. The death rattle is merely the beginning, and the road to recovery is painfully long.

•

Several days after I arrived in Port-au-Prince, I travelled to a hospital run by Médecins Sans Frontières (Doctors without Borders) where only children were treated.

The hospital was really just a damaged building with a few sheets or tarps set up to provide some shelter from the sun. Some operations had to be carried out on the dirty ground in the open air, which is where I found Bovet Yvenor. She was an eight-year-old girl who was home at the time of the quake. Bovet was crushed as her flimsy house was pancaked. She suffered terrible injuries and, I suppose, was lucky to be alive when so many others weren't. I was drawn to her by the screams. Ear-piercing screams that were followed by a deflated and exhausted cry. The whimper of a child.

A small group of people had crowded around her little body, so I walked over to see what the problem was. I wasn't expecting anything unusual because I had seen a lot of terrible things during the previous few days. But when it's a child, it's so very different. Many of the bones in her body were broken and a doctor was applying a cast. A full-body cast. I soon realised that the people who had gathered around her were not there to try and soothe her pain. They were there to hold her down. It was the only way to prevent deformity. She was only eight and so had plenty of growing to do. I noticed her right arm flailing about. So I squeezed myself into the group, knelt down beside her, and held her hand. At that precise moment there was silence, almost as if the sound from her mouth had been muted. She turned her head, which was wet from the heat and the tears, and looked directly at me.

Still silence.

As the doctor continued to wrap the cast around her, Bovet continued to look into my eyes. She appeared to be transfixed. I thought it was probably because my skin colour was white and everyone else's was black, so she may have been wondering who this unusual-looking person was. She didn't say anything, just continued to gaze. Her worried father was sitting next to me. He looked at me and said in broken English, 'Thank you. I think she likes you,' which was followed by a heart-warming smile. The doctor finished the job and Bovet looked tired. I felt sorry for her because she wasn't going to be able to move much over the next few months and the hotter summer months, where temperatures reach forty degrees in Haiti, were on the way.

I shifted to the next room and found there were many others just like Bovet. Children with their own heartbreaking stories of survival that would come to define the disaster for me.

'I've never seen anything like this,' an American doctor told me. 'You've got six people lined up here with amputations. They're septic and are going to die, even with antibiotics, if they don't have amputations and there's no place to send them.'

I wish I could have spoken to the patients but none of them spoke English and I couldn't speak Creole or French, the common languages of Haiti.

We filmed a small boy in a separate room. He had just woken up and was lying on a thin blanket on top of the concrete floor. He was seven years old and one of his legs had been removed just above the knee. The little stump that remained was heavily bandaged with a shade of claret coming through the white material. He leaned up and gazed around, probably trying to make sense of his surroundings. His name was Ferguson. But despite the fact that he'd lost one of his legs and wouldn't be able to run or play soccer anymore, he didn't seem overly concerned. He asked for the doctor, who put his ear to the boy's mouth, and Ferguson whispered something. The doctor looked at him and then looked at me. I asked him what was said.

'Can I go home yet?' was what the boy asked.

I was stunned.

Not a cry. Not a complaint. Not even a request for water. He just wanted to go home.

Ferguson was perhaps too young to realise what had happened to his home, which had probably collapsed. But there was more. His parents had been killed. He just didn't know it yet. How do you even explain that to a child after such a tragedy?

One of the American doctors told me, 'The main thing I've learned from Haiti and these people here: you don't know what you don't know, and you don't know what you don't have.'

Whenever things become tough for me I think of Bovet and Ferguson. Two children who battled through an extraordinarily difficult situation and dealt with it. But Bovet and Ferguson were not the only victims – they were just two who I came across in a city that had been wiped out, lost to Mother Nature's evil streak. There's no way of knowing for sure, but the death toll was estimated to be more than 250,000 people.

More than 250,000 dead.

That's about the same as Indonesia's Boxing Day tsunami. The people of Haiti had paid a huge price for being poor. For living on top of each other in shanties and tightly packed buildings, and for living on a fault line. Now they had to rebuild. In my experience, the bravest of people come from the poorest of nations, but I found it difficult to imagine how the people of Haiti were going to bounce back. It was going to take a long time. Years later, the nation still hasn't recovered. Most of the money to rebuild has come from foreign aid, but the process has been dogged by economic mismanagement courtesy of a corrupt government.

Haiti broke my heart. I still think about it today. I think about Ferguson and Bovet. I wonder what they're doing now. How they remember January 2010. Their stories were heartbreaking but they showed me that, out of the dark pit of fear and despair, hope can be reborn.

Chapter 9

TROUBLE WITHIN

I couldn't escape a single thought. Bodies pulled from debris, lifeless children zipped up in bags, bloated faces and missing limbs. A mother's cry, a child's scream. A charred corpse lying on the ground, alone, away from the family he or she may have had. Dark and disturbing images flashed across my mind like a short traumatic film on repeat. All the death and chaos that I had seen on the road rushed back over me like a tidal wave.

I was on holiday in Spain towards the end of 2011, a year that had ranked as one of the most brutal in recent history. Wars, conflicts, massacres, bloody revolutions, riots and upheaval, and I had been at the centre of many of them.

It was a clear sunny day. A real five-star sparkler where the sky is the bluest of blues and the trees are the greenest of greens. I walked around Madrid, photographing the beautiful royal palaces, and the centuries-old sandstone monuments. Then out of nowhere, panic set in.

I have a small spot on my leg that's been there for twenty years, but all of a sudden I thought it was skin cancer and I was going to die. Rather dramatic, I know, but it was the trigger that led to more drastic thoughts. I started worrying about my own mortality and that film in my head began to play again. Any rational thought fled my brain as if it had no place there anymore. With quick steps and quick breaths, I walked several kilometres back to my hotel room, locked myself in and didn't leave for twenty-four hours.

The film in my head played on and on. I tried reading – didn't work. I played music, loudly – no change. I stood in the shower for about an hour but still the thoughts consumed me. There was no one to talk to, no one to ask what the hell was happening to me. I ended up phoning my mum, who is a trained counsellor, and she told me that the brain is like a filing cabinet and, without me even knowing it, my brain was constantly storing pages and pages of information – sights, sounds, and smells. But there can come a point where the cabinet can't store any more information and the pages burst out. My mental pages were filled with images of horror and misery. The garbage trucks filled with Haiti's dead, the warplanes and missiles from Libya and Egypt, the mayhem of a burning London, the insanity of a lone gunman terrorising Oslo, it was all there. Was it post-traumatic stress? Or a panic attack? Or was I just burnt out? I couldn't understand it. I was only twenty-nine and I was enjoying my work. I felt physically and mentally ripe. But I was consumed with thoughts of my own mortality.

I managed to feel a little better the next day and so finished my holiday in Spain, but flying in a plane became a major mental hurdle. It had never been a problem before. In fact, quite the contrary. I enjoyed being on flights because I couldn't be contacted and could peacefully prepare for the story I was flying in to. There were even occasions when I may have been the calmest passenger on board. Once I was in a single-engine plane and not wearing a seatbelt when we hit an air pocket and sharply dropped altitude. I crashed against the ceiling and landed back in my seat, but rather than freak out I laughed for the rest of the flight. After Spain, I longed for that mindset!

But after Spain, I thought that the more I flew the greater my chances were of getting on a plane that was going to crash into a mountain or an ocean. I flew a lot – more than a hundred times every year. Short flights. Long flights. Bumpy flights. Smooth flights. My air mile programs were in great shape. Pity my head wasn't. But I kept my new fears secret. I couldn't let them control me because my job was too important and I loved it more than I hated flying. So I just had to cop it.

I was a nervous wreck for most of every flight for the rest of that year, which provided ample entertainment to my cameraman James Gillings. He would often chuckle at my expense, but there were no hard feelings; I probably would have done the same to him. The slightest hint of turbulence and I would grip the armrests tightly. I would constantly scan the cabin to see if any other passengers looked bothered. They never did. I felt every bump and every sway of the plane. Sweat would pour from my forehead and palms. I listened very carefully to every word that was uttered by the captain, and paid close attention to the movements of the attendants to see if anything was unusual. It was utterly ridiculous because if the plane went down, what was I going to do? Save it? Maybe it was a control issue, or a loss of it. I couldn't properly watch the in-flight entertainment because I couldn't enjoy it. Reading books was always interrupted by those damned air pockets outside. Even eating was a chore because my stomach was tied up in knots.

It was a tremendous relief whenever the plane I was on landed. I had survived the safest mode of transport. *Hallelujah!* But towards the end of any trip, the fear would creep in once more. I would start to think about the bloody return flight home, knowing that I would have to deal with my head again at 38,000 feet.

I became obsessed with the finest details of every plane crash. I couldn't help but feel for the passengers and wondered what those final horrifying moments had been like. Imagine not being able to say goodbye to your friends and family. I combed over every detail and development of the doomed Air France flight 447 that crashed into the Atlantic in 2009, which I reported on from the United States. Coincidentally, my brother Karl filed a terrific report on the disaster for *60 Minutes,* which I was glued to, and I peppered him for details after it aired. The plane had left Rio de Janeiro bound for Paris but flew into bad weather and crashed in the Atlantic due to a fatal mixture of mechanical malfunction and pilot error. It was an absolute tragedy. I often put myself in the shoes of those passengers and wondered how they felt and what they thought as the plane plunged into the ocean. It was totally counterproductive to my own fears, but my old friend *rational thought* still hadn't fully come back to me.

A few years after the incident in Spain, I had to fly into beautiful Venice for a story. We travelled at night through a storm and, as the captain prepared for a bumpy descent, there was a huge bang, like a loud crack, and the windows were lit up by a bright flash on both sides of the cabin. I was trying to read a book and the noise frightened the hell out of me. My heart just about leapt right out of my mouth. *Is this it?* I wondered. *See,* I told myself, *I knew I would die in a plane crash!* It was dark so I couldn't see what had happened. Was the plane still intact? Was the luggage tumbling out of the storage area? Were we all about to be sucked out of the plane? I kicked around some pretty drastic images. There was silence from the cockpit for another ten minutes or so, which confirmed my worst thoughts. *The pilot must be trying to work out what to do to save the plane and us,* I told myself. My wonderful Italian translator Giulia Sirignani was on the plane and she was as startled as I was, looking around for any sign of trouble. At least I wasn't alone.

The captain broke his silence a short time later with a casual message on the PA system that went something like this: 'Folks, this is, ahhh, your captain speaking. You may, ahhh, have noticed a loud noise a little earlier, which was, ahhh, followed by a bright light. We were in fact just struck by lightning. But there is, ahhh, no reason to be alarmed. It's actually quite regular that planes get hit by lightning and, ahhh, it shouldn't cause, ahhh, any damage because the modern day aircraft has been tested and, ahhh, built to deal with these random acts of nature. We are now continuing our descent and, ahhh, should be on the ground in another twenty minutes or so. Thank you very much for flying with us today. It's, ahhh, been a real pleasure having you on board.'

My pulse returned to normal.

But in 2011 the fear wouldn't subside. Dark thoughts still lingered from my Spanish sojourn. When I returned to London, my friend and fellow Channel Nine correspondent Rob Penfold advised me to see a psychologist. I wasn't sure. It's not something anyone in the industry really talks about. It's sometimes incorrectly assumed that struggling with a story's aftermath makes you a weaker journalist. Not tough enough to deal with the hard stuff. At least that's what I thought.

The doctor I saw told me that the two most common stories discussed in her room by the journalists she saw at that time were the Libyan war and the Haitian earthquake. Most of her journalist patients had been to one or the other. I had been to both. We went through some exercises to restore order in my head. I was asked to tap my kneecaps repeatedly while describing the worst of the images. I'm not sure what the point of the exercise was but the doc was the professional so I went along with it. I was asked to describe everything, from the darkest of the dark to the worst of the worst. *What did you see? How did you feel?* It was strange for me not to be the one asking questions. I spoke of the things I saw, and the people I spoke to, including all the violent sounds and the sickly smells. She kept probing until I couldn't remember any more. She told me she regularly saw war reporters and it was nothing to be ashamed of, that it was perfectly natural to have constant flashbacks, which I did. If I heard a loud sound like a car backfiring, I would jump and my mind would race back to North Africa. That still happens, even today. She told me I needed rest, and probably to talk to someone at home if I could. But there was the rub. As a correspondent I lived mostly on my own, so I never had anyone to discuss the life-threatening situations I had been in or the long arduous stories I had reported on once I returned home. It stayed on my chest and in my head. Sights. Sounds. Smells. Images stewed in my mind until that filing cabinet had burst open in Spain.

There is a scene in the brilliant film *The Hurt Locker* where the lead character, played by Jeremy Renner, returns home to America from the war in Iraq and finds himself at a supermarket trying to select what cereal to buy. It was a scene that I could relate to. I'm not suggesting my experiences were even close to those of serving soldiers on the frontline, but after being in conflicts where decisions are made that could potentially mean life or death, returning home to choose what to eat seems utterly insignificant.

Returning to 'normal society' after a violent news story can be a tricky adjustment. Not many people understand what you might have just seen. How would someone in Westminster know what it's like in Benghazi or Mariupol? Who wants to hear about death and misery at the dinner table? As proud as I was of my job and the stories I aired, it was easier to stay hidden for a few days when I returned home. I preferred to lie on the couch and watch films until I was called to my next assignment, which usually wasn't that long. Maybe that was the issue in 2011, because the big ugly stories happened back to back to back. There was no rest. No time to decompress. It all built up. Decompression is a term many journalists use when they return home after covering a story that involves deep mental and emotional pressure. Perhaps it's similar to a diver plunging to new depths. Often we come home as a different person to the one who left because of what we've seen or heard or felt. The pressure valve in your head needs to be readjusted. Rest is usually what's needed, and to talk (usually to those people who've had the same experiences), but it takes time to ease back into society. You can't force it either. Decompression can take days, weeks, months, or even years.

I only had one session with the psychologist. I was comforted by the fact that I wasn't the only journalist who needed to talk to someone. Mental cabinet restored. I actually felt that the session made me a better reporter because afterwards I knew how to mentally compartmentalise, and to decompress when the cameras stopped rolling. I had a better idea of when to keep going, and when to turn back. And if other people had problems, or new and young cameramen came along, then I had some experience to draw on in order to help them.

Sometimes I would burst into spontaneous fits of laughter at the absurdity of some of the situations my cameramen and I found ourselves in. One week James Gillings and I were in the Middle East being threatened with machetes or grenades, the next we were at a royal wedding discussing the intricacies of royal protocol and tradition. Humour often pulled us through.

Being a foreign correspondent is truly the greatest profession and I always regarded my time travelling the world as a great privilege. I was lucky to be covering the biggest world events in recent history. I put my heart into every single story I told and worked hard to air as much as I could. That, to me, was important. The stories needed to be told, and I believe Australians are intelligent people who want to know what is going on in the rest of the world because we live so far away.

My time as a correspondent was not just a privilege, but also a real-life thrill ride. An adventure that I was always seeking. Breaking international news from one country to the next – I loved it.

•

I come from a family of travellers. It's in my blood to be a searcher. I've always been curious about what lies beyond. To cross a border, see a culture, adapt, then do it again. The origins of the surname Stefanovic come from the former Yugoslavia, now Serbia, which in itself suggests my forebears covered a great distance to get here.

The short but no less incredible version of my family's story starts with my grandfather Dragic Stefanovic, who was born in a small town called Gložane near the Yugoslav capital of Belgrade. As a 20-year-old soldier with the Yugoslav army, he was captured by the Germans in 1939 and kept as a prisoner of war just months after World War II began. The story of his capture, as told by my dad, goes like this. As bullets flew through the air my grandfather had been shouting orders at a small group of fellow officers from the top of a hill for them to fire at the encroaching German army. He stood next to a machine-gunner, who'd stopped shooting. My frustrated grandfather pulled his handgun out of his holster and said to the gunner, 'If you don't start firing I will shoot you!' But as he raised his gun to the man's head, the machine-gunner's body slumped to the side – he'd already been killed by the German bullets.

'Deda', as we called him, was a prisoner in northern Germany for most of the war, and while he was there he met a German woman named Elisabet Henze, who had been married to an officer of the SS who was killed in battle in Scandinavia. Elisabet risked her own life by tossing food such as potatoes, carrots and other vegetables wrapped in knotted towels to Dragic over the prison fence at night. He decided he would marry her after the war.

In the smouldering ruins of post-war Europe, they fled to a place in West Germany called Haltern, which was where my father Alexander was born. As part of Germany's punishment after the war ended, any Allied soldiers who were captured received compensation. In my grandfather's case it was the completion of a university degree in civil engineering. Once that was done the plan to emigrate was made. The only decision was: America or Australia?

When Dad was four years old they joined the great migration out of Germany, climbed aboard a boat and sailed to Bellambi, north of Wollongong. They didn't know what life in Australia would be like but they knew it had to be a damned sight safer than the continent they were leaving. They took a chance.

I had a transient childhood as I moved from school to school across the great state of Queensland, but my first major adventure came at school's end. Like my grandparents, I took a chance. I was seventeen years old with dreams of becoming a professional footballer in England. My dad had also played in England in his prime, and laced up with English legends including World Cup winning captain Bobby Moore at West Ham United Football Club. When I finished school, Dad phoned his old pal Harry Redknapp – the Hammers' coach at the time – and hooked me up with a trial at the club. I'd come off a big season in Brisbane and Dad thought I was ready for a crack at the big time. So I flew to England on my own. Little did I know, but at that time West Ham had the top youth squad in the whole of the United Kingdom. I trained with blokes who would one day play for England. British household names and footballing superstars such as Frank Lampard, Rio Ferdinand, Michael Carrick, Jermain Defoe, Joe Cole, and Glen Johnson were all there at the same time I was. I was pretty chuffed to be in their company and tried not to stare at them in wide-eyed disbelief.

I walked out onto the training fields one morning with the club's Italian star Paolo Di Canio. There were dozens of fans and autograph hunters waiting and he stopped to greet them on the way out to the beautiful green paddocks. I couldn't help but smile at the strange world I'd found myself in. Only a few months earlier I'd been watching these players on the telly!

But here is the rub about wanting to be a football star in England, kids. Very few players make it to the top, and because spots are so scarce, rival players will do anything if their place at the club is threatened. As the new guy, I was an immediate outcast. I was excluded from groups, and whenever the coach or manager was watching I was given difficult balls to control from my 'teammates' so errors were made. This happened day after day and I was way too shy to speak up, so I found it a very isolating experience. I knew I had to raise my game to a higher level, but it was tough.

There were moments when I thought I might make it. One day I received a ball on the edge of the penalty box, and with my back to goal I turned the ball around the big defender who was right up my clacker, and with one powerful strike I fired the ball into the top right-hand corner of the goal from about twenty yards out. *Pick that out,* I thought. Lampard and Ferdinand were watching from the side and both of them cheered and applauded the move. I couldn't believe what I had actually done. It was perfect. Any player would have been happy with it. But rather than celebrate, I shrugged my shoulders and walked back to the halfway line as if I did that all the time. *Plenty more of that in my bag of tricks, coach.* There were a few other good moments like that, but I knew I wasn't as good as the players I was trying to dislodge. I gave it every chance, but by the time the trial came to an end I knew what was coming. The youth squad manager Tony Carr pulled me aside and said, 'You're a good player, son. But not good enough to make the grade I'm afraid.' That was it. Football dream over. On my way out of the training grounds, I pinched a training strip for good measure and smiled at an old black and white picture of my dad on the wall as I left. 'Good one, son,' I heard him say. A small win for me.

I suppose I could have hung around and tried for another club but I was homesick and couldn't be arsed, so I left my East London digs and travelled back to Brisbane. To be honest, I wasn't really that gutted. After a month in East London I knew deep down that playing football wasn't really what I wanted to do as a career.

Other than sport, English was the only thing I thought I was good at. My brother Karl had already embarked on a successful career as a journalist so he invited me to do some work experience with him. Like me, Karl had a thirst for the unknown and a hunger for adventure.

Professionally, Karl is one of the hardest-working men I know, and that serves as an inspiration to me. Privately, like my sister Elisa and my younger brother Tom, he's obscenely loyal. A very generous and supportive brother who has served as one of my mentors over the years, alongside Robert Penfold. In my opinion, Karl is one of the best broadcasters in Australian television history, an annoyingly skilful athlete across many different codes, and a good-time fella. Sometimes it is forgotten just how good a journalist Karl is and how much he cares for the profession.

I love the game of football, but I'm glad my time at West Ham didn't work out. Because, despite a few mental hiccups I've had along the way, I am so thankful to work as a journalist and the adventure I've been on as a foreign correspondent is incomparable.

Chapter 10

2013: A SOUTH AFRICAN ODYSSEY

OSCAR PISTORIUS AND NELSON MANDELA ──────

Oscar Pistorius sobbed in the court. He was hunched over on a wooden chair, making minimal eye contact during the bail hearing, which was his first court appearance since his arrest for the murder of his girlfriend Reeva Steenkamp on 15 February 2013. Pistorius, the famous Olympian, was dressed in a black suit, a light blue shirt, and a dark tie – far different from the grey hoodie he had been arrested in the previous morning.

'Take it easy,' Magistrate Desmond Nair told him.

The heat inside the Pretoria courthouse was stifling. It was the middle of a South African summer. There was no air-conditioning – just red brick walls, no open windows, and loads of people. People who'd come for a gander, because the court case was already the talk of the town. It was South Africa's OJ Simpson trial. The rumour and gossip mills were charging along at a rate of knots. There was chatter in the barber shops, chatter amongst the roadside fruit stands, and vegetable sellers were arguing with newsagents. 'He did it,' one would say. 'No way, he's innocent,' said another. People came up to me and asked, 'Have you heard? Oscar Pistorius killed his girlfriend.' Yes, I'd heard. Could I believe it? Did I know what had happened? The arrest stunned the country, and the world followed suit. People would pore over every detail. Strangers would stand near me during my live crosses back to Australia and listen in to my reports.

During the bail hearing, the courtroom was filled with people – family members, friends, lawyers, journalists and ordinary South Africans who got in early for a seat. Those who couldn't find room inside gathered outside; it was a fascinating sight as large groups of people squeezed past each other and climbed over one another for a peek. They took turns watching developments through the small glass window panel that was built into the middle of a large wooden entrance door. They wanted to see the man in question; the man who was rapidly tumbling in a sudden fall from grace. Oscar Pistorius – the double amputee known as 'the Blade Runner' who gave hope to many by becoming the first Paralympian in history to compete at an able-bodied Olympic Games.

All anybody knew in the early stages was that Oscar Pistorius and his beautiful girlfriend, Reeva Steenkamp, were at his place on the night of Valentine's Day. The last images of her alive showed her driving her Mini Cooper hatchback into his gated compound. She was smiling and laughing with the main guard; no outward signs of trouble or fear of what might lie ahead. She had just finished a yoga class, and he watched TV until they went to bed. The couple slept together in the bedroom on the second floor, but during the night she locked herself in the bathroom nearby, which was where she was shot dead.

South Africa is one of the most violent countries on earth; a place where murder, assault, rape, robbery, kidnap, and theft happen daily. Oscar slept without his prosthetic legs on, but always kept them close by. During the night, he heard a noise, which was probably his girlfriend in the bathroom. He claimed he thought it was an intruder and so immediately felt vulnerable to attack. He picked up a handgun that he kept by his bedside, moved to the bathroom door, and fired his gun four times. When he bashed the locked door open, he found his blood-soaked girlfriend slumped on the floor. The only witnesses were neighbours, some of whom claimed to have heard yelling in the hours leading up to Reeva's death. Oscar phoned a friend, and then phoned police as he carried Reeva's body down the staircase to the ground floor – which is where she was found by police when they arrived. Pistorius was taken to Pretoria Police Station and, hours later, was charged with murder.

At the time, I had one question – one that many people had – and I still have it today. If you heard a noise and thought it was an intruder, why wouldn't you check where your girlfriend was before you fired your gun?

•

Oscar Pistorius was a big deal in South Africa. He was a national icon, cherished alongside Nelson Mandela and the Springboks. His was a rags-to-riches tale that was all the more inspiring because his goals were achieved without legs.

Pistorius was born in November 1986 without the fibula bone in each of his legs and the whole lateral side of his foot was also missing, so all he had were two toes and the bones on the inside of his foot and heel. His challenging start to life was also difficult for his parents who were now faced with a major decision: reconstruct or amputate? Understandably, it was a hugely emotional call but after some debate it was decided the child would lose his legs.

Oscar didn't just overcome his handicap, he excelled on the track and the rugby field as well. The fearless teenager even waterskied. In later interviews, he said he put much of his determination down to the endless encouragement of his mother. Sadly, she died when he was fifteen so she never got to see him realise his athletic potential, but Oscar still used her as inspiration.

In 2004, he competed in the Athens Paralympics. Four years later, he was at Beijing where he became a symbol of the Paralympic Games and was given the nickname Blade Runner. But Oscar wanted more; he wanted to compete against the able-bodied athletes at the Olympics in London. To do so, he had to fight a ban by the Olympic committee, which claimed the high-tech carbon-racing blades he used gave him an unfair advantage. Eventually he won the right to compete.

Pistorius went to London as one of the most hyped stars. I was among Channel Nine's reporting team for the games and we were well aware of the unique power of his story and so covered it extensively. Already he had done what no other disabled athlete had done before – competed at an Olympic Games. When he hit the track, he was inspiring. So good that he made it through to the semi-finals of the 400 metres. He topped it all off by carrying the South African flag at the closing ceremony. He went on to win gold and silver medals at the Paralympics. His fan base couldn't get enough, including the women. Pistorius was known as a player who dated several beautiful women. After the London games, his fame and his looks made him irresistible, which brings us to Reeva Steenkamp.

If Pistorius was the David Beckham of South African sport in that he was so highly revered, Steenkamp was the Victoria Beckham in that she also had a high profile. She was a 29-year-old law graduate turned bikini model who'd just finished a popular reality TV show, *Tropika Island of Treasure*.

During the bail hearing I flew down to Cape Town to interview Reeva's uncle, Michael Steenkamp. The murder case had received so much traction in Australia that I was asked to put together a documentary on the fallen star for

Channel Nine, with the help of producers Hamish Thompson and Wes Hardman.

Reeva's father Barry was too distraught to speak on camera, but his brother Michael allowed cameraman James Gillings and me into his home.

'I have my moments of breaking down. It's hard. It's not easy and if your emotions cry out, you must go with it. You must be able to cry,' he said.

We spoke at length about Reeva.

'She was always outgoing, always part of everything. She wanted to be a pleasing person and a loving person. I think she gave a lot to those who came close to her. She loved her family and her family loved her.'

Her relationship with Oscar had only been going for three months.

'It was a nice courtship that was taking place. They seemed fine. As fine as a courting couple would be. They seemed like a loving couple.'

To learn more about Oscar, we spoke to his family as well. His uncle, Mike Azzie, was a horse trainer outside Pretoria.

'I'd found out early in the morning and my wife burst into tears. She said to me, "Ozzie has been arrested." I asked her why. This can't be true. It just cannot be true. It's not Oscar.'

Oscar had a well-renowned dark side. He loved guns and he had applied for extra firearm licences in the months leading up to Reeva's shooting. His uncle tried to explain.

'You know, he's like any of us. We all have tempers, and I'd seen his aggressive nature when he was playing outside, or when he was playing in the pool, when he was playing water polo with the boys. He would grab them and shove them under the water like they would do to him. An aggressive side, but nothing that would be untoward.'

Pistorius was a hero to many. I went to Soweto, the township south-west of Johannesburg, where I found a running club. All the junior athletes were practising. I asked them what they thought of Pistorius. One of the young girls said, 'Oscar Pistorius is the fastest runner of South Africa even though he doesn't have legs.'

The head coach then told me, 'I'm very, very sad because this guy is my role model.'

•

Police found a nine-millimetre pistol and an assault rifle at Oscar's house after it became a crime scene. The first officer in the house was a chap named Detective Hilton Botha. He was a star witness for the state during the bail hearing, which lasted four days. Detective Botha claimed to have found two boxes of testosterone and needles in Pistorius's room. That would certainly fit the theory that Pistorius was injecting himself with a possible performance-enhancing drug, which may have led to fits of rage. But that argument was shot down by defence lawyers who claimed the testosterone was just a herbal remedy.

Then Detective Botha, the star witness, named two neighbours who heard arguments and gunshots at the time Reeva was killed. One neighbour heard 'screams and loud arguments coming from the house in the hour before the shots were fired'. Then there was the second neighbour who heard 'two bursts of gunfire with seventeen minutes of silence in-between'. That didn't bode well for the defence either, until it was revealed the neighbours weren't really close neighbours – they lived 300 metres away. So those sounds could have been anything coming from anywhere. The twists and turns kept the story high in the news agenda for news teams across the world. Every day brought a new stunning revelation. Every day there was a new angle and it was a unique and exhilarating reporting experience. Court proceedings began about half an hour before my live crosses into the evening news, which meant I often had new developments and morsels of intrigue that were added to the story for our viewers at home. It was the kind of story where people wanted more information. Also, because Channel Nine, along with the ABC, were the only Australian TV news crews there, it made it that much better to cover.

One example of a late and dramatic development was when it was revealed in court that star witness Detective Botha had a problem of his own. He was facing seven attempted murder charges for firing his gun at a bus two years earlier. It was also argued that he had contaminated the crime scene with unprotected shoes, and lost track of illegal ammunition found in Oscar's house. The star witness was no more. He had become a liability for the state, so he was kicked off the case.

The outlook was starting to look a little less bleak for Pistorius. He was crying less and less. Until the case took another turn, but this twist didn't relate to him. Since Oscar's arrest, his brother Carl had led his cheer squad. He came to court every day making sure his brother was well supported. He wasn't a huge fan of the media interest, although there wasn't a thing that could be done about that. Oscar was still in police custody, and was driven to and from court every day in police cars, rather than walking through the press scrums as he did during his trial. So I asked Carl a few questions at court from time to time, which always went unanswered. Just before my broadcast one day, towards the end of the hearing, news broke from South African media that Carl had been in a bit of trouble himself a few years back. In fact, two days before Reeva Steenkamp's death, Carl Pistorius was in court on a manslaughter charge relating to the death of a female motorcyclist. While not relating to Oscar's murder case, it was a blow for the family, and Oscar's tears were back.

Oscar Pistorius didn't take the stand during his bail hearing – that would come the following year during his well-publicised murder trial. Instead, with the help of his lawyer, Barry Roux, he submitted an affidavit to the court. The fact that Oscar killed Reeva Steenkamp wasn't in question. It was all about whether he meant to. After outlining his assets, which included three properties, and an estimated income of about AU$600,000 per year, he launched into his version of events, insisting he had thought there had been an intruder in the bathroom.

I have kept all of my notebooks from my years abroad and have a few dedicated to the case of Pistorius. On one of my pages there is a quote attributed to Prosecutor Gerrie Nel: 'He shot and killed an innocent woman. She was shot four times as she was behind the bathroom door. There is no possible explanation to support Pistorius's claim that he thought Reeva was an intruder. In fact, claiming Reeva was an intruder was part of the plan.'

Prosecutor Nel didn't buy the affidavit and ultimately asked, 'Why would a burglar lock themselves in a bathroom? And why was Reeva's mobile phone in the toilet at 3 am?'

The magistrate thought they were worthy questions, among many others, to explore, so he agreed Pistorius should face the most serious charge – premeditated murder – and the case would go to trial.

•

A year would pass before the trial was finally underway. Pistorius was allowed out on bail and spent the time at his uncle's mansion in Pretoria. He returned to training, but had lost a lot of weight.

I felt sympathy for the family of Reeva Steenkamp. Her parents had had to bury their only child and were doing it tough – physically, mentally, and financially. I didn't cover the trial, which was covered by my colleague Tom Steinfort, but I watched on with interest. I couldn't quite believe the eventual verdict in which Pistorius was found guilty of culpable homicide, which meant he only had to spend a few months behind bars. This was later appealed though and Pistorius has since been found guilty of murder. At the time of writing, Pistorius is still before the courts, due to be sentenced in June 2016.

It wasn't long before I was back in South Africa though.

•

I needed a break. It was June 2013 and it had already been a busy year. Like a footballer waiting for the referee to blow his whistle to signify half-time, I too was ready to trudge off to the change rooms for a rest. There was Pistorius in South Africa, the historic and unexpected resignation of Pope Benedict XVI and the papal conclave in Rome, the premiere in Cannes of Australian film *The Great Gatsby*, Margaret Thatcher's death and her state funeral in London, British Fusilier Lee Rigby's murder on the street by extremists, and Anzac Day at Villers-Bretonneux – all big stories crammed into a short space of time.

The Glastonbury music festival was three days away. As a music lover and poor amateur musician, I had always wanted to go. I had a ticket and was preparing to join friends on the muddy fields of Somerset. The Rolling Stones were headlining. So were the Arctic Monkeys. One of the old English greats and one of the modern English greats together on the same bill. Just the tonic I needed to hit the reset button.

The news gods had other ideas.

It was a Sunday evening and I'd just watched a film at home when a news banner flashed across the bottom of the screen: 'Nelson Mandela rushed to hospital in critical condition.' We had already been to Johannesburg in April that year for a false alarm about Mandela, but there was no question the old warrior was running out of fight. Mandela was ninety-four years old and hadn't been seen in public in years. Glastonbury was gone.

James and I boarded a plane to Johannesburg and focused on the job ahead.

Mandela managed to pull through once again, but his body was at an advanced age and was slowly failing him. He had a recurring lung infection that was brought on by the tuberculosis he'd suffered as he worked the lime quarry as a political prisoner on Robben Island. Mandela had state-of-the-art medical facilities at his home in Johannesburg, but after his frequent health scares I often wondered why his family didn't just let him go. He was clearly shutting down. But I guess I would want to hang on to a family member for as long as possible if I were in that position.

This was an important story to cover. Still, it sure would have been nice to check out the Stones!

•

A news conference was set for late evening on 5 December 2013. South African President Jacob Zuma would appear. The topic would be Nelson Mandela. There was no official word on what had happened, or what was happening, but everyone assumed Mandela's time had come. My producer Eliza Berkery had already booked Luke Wilson and me on a twelve-hour flight from London to Johannesburg. A smart move. It was tough to get seats because Britain's huge press packs were trying to do the same thing. Then a few hours later came the confirmation:

> My fellow South Africans, our beloved Nelson Rolihlahla Mandela, the founding president of our democratic nation, has departed. He passed on peacefully in the company of his family around 8.50 pm on 5 December 2013. He is now resting. He is now at peace. Our nation has lost its greatest son. Our people have lost a father. Although we knew that this day would come, nothing can diminish our sense of a profound and enduring loss. His tireless struggle for freedom earned him the respect of the world.

Jacob Zuma is far from the most popular president in South African history – even Mandela was known to have been a critic, disappointed that Zuma didn't carry on with what Mandela set out to achieve – but everyone shared the grief. Indeed, it was global. Nelson Mandela was undoubtedly one of the most famous people in the world; he was certainly the most revered.

I arrived to find a nation's grief on full display. My first stop was at Mandela's home in Johannesburg, where a floral shrine made up of flowers, notes, and candles was growing by the minute. There was a line-up of news cameras using the shrine as a backdrop, which I quickly joined to file my first live report – the first of dozens that would come over the next ten days. I had long admired Mandela and read quite a few books on his life and legacy. I had also filmed a documentary on him earlier in the year for Channel Nine, so I was armed with plenty of information.

But it was the South African people who gave us the best idea of who Mandela was and what he meant. Thousands of them gathered at his home. Many stood with their heads bowed and said a quiet prayer, but most of them joined together in song. When African voices unite in harmony, it creates a sound that is so powerful it gives your entire body goose bumps. I had no idea what the words were they were singing, but it was almost as if I was listening to a celestial choir.

•

He seemed shorter than I imagined him to be. But even in death, Nelson Mandela had an aura about him. The short silver hair, the patterned silk shirt that had become his uniform, the lines on his face marked by his long years of experience – the happy times and the sad times. His eyes were closed, and although he was at peace, I didn't feel he looked it. He had something of a concerned appearance. Maybe it was down to the health struggles of his final years. Maybe he was just a tired old man having a deserved rest. The old warrior had fought the battle of life, and finally decided he'd had enough.

As his lifelong friend and former Robben Island prisoner Mac Maharaj told me when I interviewed him for the Mandela documentary, 'I think Madiba lived at times through sheer willpower. At the end of the day he lived as long as he enjoyed life, and I think at that moment when he thought, well, it's time to go, he went.'

I only had about ten seconds to stand and look, because there was a long queue of people waiting to do the same. With the flick of a finger, security guards dressed in dark suits told mourners to quietly shuffle on. There was something morbidly curious about looking at a body in a glass-topped casket, especially when that body was a true giant of history. It was the only time I ever had the chance to see him. That fraction of a minute was all I needed to observe an extraordinary soul, and it was more than enough for mourners to quietly whisper, 'Thank you.'

Mandela's body was lying in state at Pretoria's Union Building, where Madiba – which was his clan name – had governed as president some twenty years prior. The mark of the man, and his legacy, was clear from the sheer volume of people who lined up in the hot sun to see him. Elders from Johannesburg were joined by the youth from Cape Town, mums and dads from Durban joined politicians and the many different tribal leaders as his supporters from right around the nation flew in to say goodbye. Tributes came in from the world's great and good.

'He is a personal hero. His legacy is one that will linger on throughout the ages,' said US President Barack Obama from Washington. He then flew to Soweto where he gave a speech at Mandela's public memorial at Soccer City Stadium, which was also the site of the 2014 World Cup Final.

From Sydney, then Australian Prime Minister Tony Abbott said, 'Mandela is someone who suffered but was not embittered but ennobled through that suffering.'

'Nelson Mandela was not just a hero of our time, but a hero of all time,' claimed British Prime Minister David Cameron from Downing Street in London.

While his eventual death had been expected, people still reacted differently to the emotional surge that seeing his body created. Some just looked or bowed, said a prayer, and then passed through. Others, however, weren't quite ready for a nation without him in it, and so tears streamed down their distraught faces. This was the scene at Pretoria's Union Building for three days.

Nelson Mandela had written about his long walk to freedom; now he was being given a long goodbye. Ten days of national mourning to farewell South Africa's favourite son.

There were the initial days of grief, followed by his body lying in state; then there was the public memorial at Soccer City Stadium (also memorable for the sign-language interpreter who was claimed to be a fake). His body was then taken on the long journey from Johannesburg to Qunu in the Eastern Cape province, which was where Mandela was born and where he'd always wanted to be buried, alongside his ancestors.

Qunu is every bit as beautiful as Mandela described in his autobiography, *Long Walk to Freedom*. It's largely dominated by beautiful green rolling hills, which became more spectacular at sunset. Families still lived there in old huts, and kids played football with bare feet. I doubt it's changed that much over the years, except for a large bitumen road that now passes right through town to the new Mandela museum.

I had spent some time up in Qunu earlier in 2013 for the documentary on the life of Mandela, which Channel Nine aired on the evening he passed away. That documentary remains one of the projects I'm most proud to have been involved in. Shooting it took us from Mandela's birthplace in Qunu, to Johannesburg and Cape Town, and out to Robben Island where he spent most of his twenty-seven years behind bars. There I met a very animated old jailer named Christo Brand who gave us a private tour of the island, the lime quarry where the prisoners worked in the hot sun, the prison yard, and Mandela's small cell.

'Mandela was always on time. He was quite disciplined, down to earth, and a humble person. You wouldn't even believe he was a leader at that point. He was a model prisoner,' Christo told me as we stood in his cell.

Mac Maharaj, Mandela's friend, painted a grisly picture for me of life on the island, especially the many long hours spent crushing rocks at the quarry or in the prison yard under a blistering hot sun. 'I don't think it was the toughness of the physical side of the labour that was painful. I think it was the monotony and it was the sense that you were expending your labour in a useless purpose. They just wanted to break your spirit.'

I often get asked who my favourite interviewee has been so far in my career. I've been lucky enough to spend time with world leaders, business icons, famous athletes, the most successful bands in history, and Hollywood's biggest and best from the silver screen. But my favourite interview to date is the one I did with political scientist Charles Villa-Vicencio. Charles has spent a lifetime studying his native South Africa, and knew how to perform for the camera.

'Mandela was dynamic, powerful, and charismatic. Throughout all of his time [incarcerated] he was not prepared to roll over, to submit. It was the vision. It was the commitment. It was the moral anticipation that sustained him and because it sustained him, it sustained all of us. He was a remarkable man. He is the epitome of what in our better moments we believe South Africa should be,' Charles told me.

I was also able to speak to Pik Botha, who was South Africa's foreign minister in the last years of the apartheid era. Mr Botha was very close to Mandela and the two often spoke on the phone as Mandela prepared to eventually leave prison. After Mandela broke up with his wife Winnie he called Pik and cried on the phone. Even the most remarkable giants of history have moments of weakness. Pik passed his stories on to me.

He cherished the ideal of a democratic and free South Africa. Equal opportunity. No domination of one race by others. I thank God he did achieve it while he was alive.

•

Military helicopters circled low as huge crowds lined the roads that led to Qunu. Men and women, boys and girls, they all danced on the street as they sang songs from the Mandela era. It was 14 December 2013 and I stood on the roof of our van along with cameraman Luke Wilson as we waited for the funeral motorcade to pass us. We needed a good vantage point to film a piece to camera. We sat for hours in the hot sun and then, in the distance, we saw the flashing lights. There was only one opportunity to get our shot before the motorcade sped past on its way to the burial site for the funeral the next day. Dozens of police vehicles supported the funeral procession on its final stretch. Luke locked his camera on the hearse, which had the coffin inside draped in the South African flag. I spoke about the mourning period coming to an end, and while it was still a sad time, people thought it was important to also celebrate the life of a hero. As I finished my spiel, Luke returned his camera to the passing car as it sped out of frame. The timing was perfect.

The world's media was kept outside the funeral because the ceremony was filmed and aired by South African television. African presidents were in attendance, so were well-known faces such as Oprah Winfrey and Richard Branson.

Mandela was buried in a small plot next to the headstones of his ancestors, which is exactly what he wanted. South Africa is thankfully a long way from the days of apartheid but it still faces major problems. Corruption, greed and racism are all prevalent. Will the country be able to get on top of those issues without Mandela around? It's impossible to replace Madiba but others can mirror him by following a simple message about legacy that Mandela's friend Mac Maharaj told me.

Mandela is the possibility that sits in you and I. 'It's easy to make a difference to your own life but to make a difference to the lives of others is the challenge and that is in your hands,' said Mandela. That is his legacy.

Chapter 11

HURRICANE OBAMA

THE ELECTION OF BARACK OBAMA ─────────

The wind was howling and the rain was blowing in sideways. Large tree branches threatened to break off, and power lines circled like skipping ropes. It was hurricane season in America's south and I was caught in a whopper. On 13 September 2008, Hurricane Ike was barrelling in from the Gulf of Mexico with destructive winds of up to 230 kilometres an hour. Ike was a huge Category 4 storm and had already killed dozens of people in Cuba and Haiti. At the time, it was the third costliest hurricane in American history.

I was with Rich Moran, one of the great cameramen of my time, and a champion of a bloke to boot. We had made our way to Galveston on the Texas coastline as the storm approached landfall. A lone security guard had blocked off the only road leading into the port town. He waved us down and we slowed to a halt. Rich wound down the window of our SUV to talk to him.

'You can't go through here, sir,' he said.

'Why not?' Rich asked.

'It's too dangerous. I can't let anybody through.' The guard seemed serious, but there were only a few orange witches hats on the road.

The sky was a dark grey and light rain fell through the open window. With a major story to cover, Rich just looked at me, then looked at the guard, and without any more thought he stepped on the accelerator and left the security man standing behind. I could only laugh as I looked in the rear-view mirror and saw the solitary guard scratch his head, as he no doubt wondered what had just happened. We were certain Galveston's good police were too preoccupied at the time to chase after us.

The city's streets had mostly been cleared, and the area had been evacuated. More than a million people had left their homes, but about 100,000 people chose to stay. Once again, I was heading into a place when most other people were heading in the opposite direction.

There was only one hotel taking reservations, but other media crews had already booked it out, so Rich and I found ourselves a good old Best Western hotel where we could ride out the storm. The hotel was a piece of garbage, and it was already heavily damaged by the strong winds, but it was all we could find. A worker at reception said we could stay if we wanted, but none of the rooms were clean. We had to enter the room through the broken window. Even so, we were grateful for the hospitality and felt like we had lucked out, until we saw a group of people staying in other rooms who appeared to be junkies squatting.

Only twelve days earlier we'd covered Hurricane Gustav, which had pummelled the city of New Orleans – three years to the day after Hurricane Katrina had devastated it. Gustav was another big one, which again peaked at Category 4 and was responsible for the deaths of 153 people – most of whom lived in the Caribbean. In Cuba, 90,000 homes had been destroyed as Gustav passed through. It was a massive storm, and a staggering three million people evacuated New Orleans after strong warnings from the government. They feared it was Katrina Mark II, and George W. Bush definitely didn't want another one of those on his watch. But when Gustav hit the US coast, its ferocity weakened considerably and it fizzled out relatively quickly.

Ike was a different beast. The wild seas were smashing against the Texan coastline and flooding local roads. In Galveston, seafront buildings, which had once stood on stilts, had already been picked up and tossed across the roads. Large pieces of timber littered the highway as heavy rain and strong winds continued to pound us.

Just as Rich and I filed our piece for Nine News that night, the power cut out and electricity was gone. Under torchlight, we dined on water and peppered beef jerky, and listened to the weather reports from the car stereo. Fourth generation (4G) technology wasn't a thing in 2008, so mobile internet access was patchy. It was late in the evening and we needed some rest before an expected full-day shoot the next day. I was anticipating serious carnage after the storm had passed through. So we disappeared into separate rooms to try and get some sleep.

A few minutes after I put my head down, the wind really picked up. The eye of the storm must have been close. The windows of my room rattled loudly, and the bed I was in shook with the ground. I felt a slight nervousness creep in. Then tiny drops of water splashed against my head. *Uh oh*. I grew up in Cairns where cyclones were common, but this felt different. It was wilder. The city was open and unprotected by the sort of mountain ranges that guarded large parts of Far North Queensland. I reached for the flashlight that I kept on the bedside table and shone it at the ceiling. A large crack had opened up above me and water was spilling through. *Shit*, I thought. *The bloody roof is going to cave in*.

I called Rich on his mobile phone and asked him if he'd mind if I crashed in his room, as mine was a bit unsafe. I was on the second floor, while he was on the first. 'Sure thing,' he said. I moved to Rich's room but I still didn't sleep a wink – the wind was too strong and the rain so hard.

Morning took forever to arrive and when it did I walked up to my room to grab my bag so we could get going. I opened the door and was hit by a bright light. I could see parts of the grey sky as rain continued to softly fall. Parts of the ceiling and roof insulation were littered all over the room. A huge plank of wood had fallen right on the pillow where my head had been. Good thing I'd left.

I got lucky. So many people didn't. We drove around the shattered city where boats had been washed up on roads and homes had been reduced to stumps. Ike was blamed for the deaths of 195 people, 112 of whom lived in the United States. Others were killed in Cuba and Haiti as the storm system surged through the gulf.

Flooding and destruction stretched from the Bahamas to a huge section of US coastline that included the Florida panhandle, Texas, Mississippi, and Louisiana. By the time Ike fizzled out and was downgraded to a rain depression, it had ended up as far north as Canada. The damage bill was US\$40 billion; it had been the worst hurricane to ever hit Cuba.

Ike and Gustav were a brutal pair of hurricanes that left their mark on America, but they weren't the only things storming across the States in 2008.

•

Obviously Barack Obama bears no personal similarity to the destructive nature of a hurricane, but his presence *was* like a force of nature whose impact was felt not only over the United States, but across the entire world. People in New York were just as likely as those in London, or Johannesburg, or Sydney, to ask, 'Who is this Barack Obama?' The common reaction to watching him was, 'I kinda like him. He's different to the rest, ya know?' A young, confident, intelligent, charismatic senator from Chicago, Illinois, who was about to change the world. 'Change' being the operative word, as it was a central theme of his election campaign. There were stunning parallels drawn between Obama and another young, handsome, hopeful, charismatic leader who rewrote history nearly fifty years earlier: John F. Kennedy.

Of course, Obama's campaign was helped because it came at the end of a deeply troubled period in American history, and the highly flawed presidency of Republican George W. Bush. Again, that didn't just concern America, it affected the world, because the fallout of George W. Bush's time in power is still being felt today. War and economics. Like it or not, the US presidency matters, and we all pay the price for Washington's decisions.

My time as a foreign correspondent was linked to Barack Obama's presidency. He was elected president just after I started work in Channel Nine's North American bureau, my first overseas posting, and his time at the White House was to end about a year out from me finishing my work at Nine's European bureau. I covered his campaign, from senator, to Democratic nominee, to president. During my time as a correspondent, many of the stories I reported on and many of the places and conflicts I travelled to usually involved his reaction, his thoughts, and his ideas. Whether those opinions and decisions have been right is for other people to judge, but at the beginning of his campaign, it seemed everything was positive.

•

We could have been at a rock concert. We could have been at a football game. But we were crammed into a stadium to watch one man speak. There were 84,000 of us to be precise, part of a sell-out crowd on 28 August 2008 at Invesco Field – the home of the Denver Broncos NFL team – to watch Barack Obama accept the nomination of the Democratic Party, which would allow him to run for president. In the States, a candidate must be elected champion of his own party first, in what's called 'primaries', before he or she can take on the other party in the 'general election'. So there are essentially two election campaigns for the US presidency – which is why it takes so long! We had just finished the primaries, which Obama narrowly won after a bruising campaign against fellow Democrat Hillary Clinton.

It seemed as though the entire audience had been galvanised by an electric current of hope and goodwill. Obama had that effect. People bought what he was selling. Of course, the Republicans would disagree, but there were no Republicans present that night.

It was a warm summer evening. Stevie Wonder was the warm-up act. The pop star played 'Signed, Sealed, Delivered I'm Yours', which energised the crowd even more. People waved their hands and danced. It was a so-called 'Obama-rama' and, I must admit, it was hard not to get caught up in it.

My broadcast position was just in front of the main stage, and the noise was so loud that it was difficult to hear the news anchors back in Sydney. Then, as darkness fell over Denver, Barack Obama walked on stage to a rapturous applause, and accepted the Democratic Party's nomination for president. He paused for effect at the end of every sentence, which was usually met by loud cheers and applause.

> Four years ago, I stood before you and told you my story, of the brief union between a young man from Kenya and a young woman from Kansas who weren't well-off or well-known, but shared a belief that in America their son could achieve whatever he put his mind to. It is that promise that's always set this country apart, that through hard work and sacrifice each of us can pursue our individual dreams, but still come together as one American family, to ensure that the next generation can pursue their dreams, as well. That's why I stand here tonight.

It was a fine speech. His listeners clung to his every word for the best part of an hour. Obama didn't miss a beat.

I had only been in the United States for eight months or so at that stage, but what a time to be there. It was my first major story to cover, so the adrenaline was pumping and it was unforgettable. It was also confirmation that this was exactly what I wanted to do. Big-ticket kind of stuff. To be reporting part of history. I'd worked hard to get this job, so I was going to do it well. The political scene was abuzz. Obama was the first African American to have been nominated for president. As an American political junkie I watched from the stands and listened to the speeches from a great list of politicians, ex-presidents, and potential future presidents, who took to the stage during the five-day Democratic convention in Denver.

It started off with Michelle Obama, whose popularity in her own right was starting to take off. This was part of her well-received sales pitch to the nation.

> Barack doesn't care where you're from, or what your background is, or what party, if any, you belong to. See, that's just not how he sees the world. He knows that thread that connects us – our belief in America's promise, our commitment to our children's future. He knows that thread is strong enough to hold us together as one nation even when we disagree.

The big talking point throughout the convention, among the public and my fellow journalists, was what would the Clintons would say. For months leading up to the convention, Obama and Hillary Clinton had been locked in a historic and messy primary campaign against each other, as they fought right down to the wire for the party's nomination. It was box office. Many of their attacks were personal and bitter, and grudges were held. The two sides didn't trust each other, and the same could be said for their supporters. But Obama had won and he needed the support of the Clintons going into the presidential campaign, because they carried the support of millions of voters.

Bill Clinton did his bit first. It can be easy to forget just how good Clinton is on stage. Maybe he's even a finer orator than Obama. He often disregards the teleprompter and just talks ad hoc without his listeners even realising. Despite any dark personal feelings he may have held towards Obama following the heated campaign against his wife, Clinton calmed the nerves of Obama's team by endorsing him.

Was it truthful? Perhaps. Was it heartfelt? It seemed so.

Next was Hillary Clinton, and she spoke right to her supporters. They were disillusioned because they had hoped for their own piece of history; that Hillary Clinton would have won the Democratic primary and then gone on to become America's first female president. She also endorsed Obama and urged her supporters to throw their weight behind him and 'join me in working as hard for Barack Obama as you have for me'.

I suppose it can be a little disconcerting to wax lyrical for too long about politicians, but it was hard to fault their performances on stage during that week. I paid close attention to how they spoke and how they engaged with audiences and voters. Australian politics can at times seem flat and lifeless. Answers to questions can be too well rehearsed and as a result the message loses its punch. But in the USA it's oh so very different. Another great thrill for me was working alongside the big names of the American news networks. From my broadcast position I'd glance left and see Anderson Cooper and Wolf Blitzer from CNN, or Katie Couric from CBS, doing exactly the same thing as me. Then I'd glance right and see Shepard Smith from FOX, or George Stephanopoulos from ABC. These are known faces of my industry, people I'd looked up to, and now I was among them, covering the biggest story in the world at the time.

In many ways, the Democratic primary campaign was more intriguing than the general election. A man hoping to become America's first African American president, pitched against a woman hoping to become America's first female president. There hadn't been a campaign like it in history. But at that point the nation was ready for Obama, more than they were ready for Hillary Clinton, and so he had all the momentum.

But that wasn't the end of the campaign controversy. There was still plenty of meat on that bone. Because standing in Obama's way was the Republican candidate, a former Vietnam veteran, John McCain, who shook the race up even further by selecting an unknown vice presidential running mate from the state of Alaska – Governor Sarah Palin.

•

It was frustratingly hot. We were in the Nevada desert at the end of the 2008 summer. It was a Far North Queensland kind of heat. Hot and humid. I felt like I resembled one of those melting wax figures from the horror movies. I'd just flown in to Las Vegas to cover an Obama stump speech.

'Stump speech' is probably the most popular term used in an election season. It's an ordinary campaign speech performed by anyone who is running for public office, and comes from an early American custom, when candidates campaigned from town to town and stood upon a sawn-off tree stump to deliver their speech. These ain't the days of Washington and Lincoln though. This is the twenty-first century where every theme song, poster, and even people selected to stand on background stages, had been co-ordinated and carefully selected by a large team of advisors.

So there we were in the Vegas suburbs. Late for Obama's speech and locked in traffic. That was when the frustration level kicked up a notch. In the general election, both sets of candidates came with extensive security detail – Secret Service kind of stuff. Also, because Obama was African American, there were obvious concerns about his safety from extreme racist groups, and the threat of assassination was real. So whenever he travelled, traffic was halted, and phone signals were often scrambled. It was a great joy to be a part of an unfolding piece of history, but at that particular juncture, on that particular day, I was properly peeved! Glenn Edwards was my cameraman at the time, and when we finally reached the location for Obama's stump speech, we quickly parked our car, hoisted the heavy recording gear on our shoulders, and ran to the entrance.

An Obama appearance came with long queues and security pat-downs, which must have been awful for the guards dealing with an outrageously sweaty crowd. 'Heavy items in the box please, ma'am! Walk through the turnstiles, sir ... slowly! Hey you, in the red shirt, back of the line now!' The mood was similar to that at Los Angeles International Airport (LAX), or JFK in New York – tense, humourless, and tightly controlled.

Once we made it through the entrance of Bonanza High School, we dashed through the audience and made our way to the large media platform that had been set up for both local and international reporters. It was a few metres from the front of the stage. Pole position really, as journalists and cameras squeezed in next to each other. We were packed in so tightly at these events, it was sometimes difficult to concentrate and report live. Often other reporters' voices could be picked up on my microphone, and vice versa. Bruce Springsteen's song 'The Rising' was playing through the loudspeakers, which meant Obama was about to step on stage.

The candidates kept a heck of a schedule in the closing stages of the general election. That morning Obama had given a televised speech in Reno, Nevada. Now he was in the Las Vegas valley, but not for long. Shortly he'd be back in his campaign plane, en route to Albuquerque, New Mexico, for another televised speech that evening.

In Las Vegas he bounced on to the stage, with a white shirt rolled up at the sleeves, blue tie and no jacket. It was too hot for that. The crowd responded with deafening cheers as they waved cards carrying the words 'Hope' and

'Change'. These had been handed out at the entrance. It was all for the cameras.

Obama's target was no longer Hillary Clinton, it was Republican rival John McCain, and as usual he laced his soaring rhetoric with subtle humour.

In what may be the strangest twist of this very strange election, Senator McCain said that I would somehow continue the Bush economic policies, and that he – John McCain – would change them. He denounced the president for letting things get completely out of hand; that's what he said. John McCain has been really angry about George Bush's economic policies, except during the primary when he said 'we've made great economic progress under George Bush,' or just last month when he said that 'the fundamentals of our economy are strong under George Bush,' or the fact that he adopted all of George Bush's policies for his own campaign. In fact, John McCain is so opposed to George Bush's policies that he voted with him ninety percent of the time for the past eight years! That's right, he really decided to stick it to George Bush ten percent of the time! Let me tell you, John McCain attacking George Bush for his out-of-hand economic policies, is like Dick Cheney attacking George Bush for his go-it-alone foreign policy. It's like Tonto attacking the Lone Ranger!

Throughout Obama's campaign in the general election, he repeated often the words 'John McCain', 'George W. Bush' and 'economics', and continued to link all three. It was a smart play. At the time, the United States was in financial turmoil as the Global Financial Crisis began to take hold. All Obama had to do was remind the public that the nation was in the crisis because of the Bush government, and if they elected John McCain it'd be more of the same. McCain knew it too, which is why he rarely quoted George W. Bush or used him during his campaign.

In the final, frantic three weeks of the general election, I crisscrossed America with cameraman Glenn Edwards. We followed the McCain–Palin rallies, while Rob Penfold and Rich Moran covered the Obama–Biden movements. I may not have been following the main star at the business end of the election, but it was an experience and a thrill all the same. We moved from airport to hotel to rally, back to hotel, then on to airport. Repeat. One day I was in Omaha, Nebraska, the next I was in Manchester, New Hampshire. From city to city, state to state – Cincinnati to Boston, Raleigh in North Carolina to the twin cities of Minnesota. I saw parts of America that I wouldn't ordinarily have visited.

The surprise selection of Sarah Palin as John McCain's running mate energised the red Republican states and gave them hope that they might pull off an unlikely election win. Palin became an even bigger star than McCain. Her rallies were much more popular than his and, all of a sudden, there seemed a chance that Palin might smash the so-called glass ceiling before Hillary Clinton did. It was certainly a different crowd. I think part of Palin's popularity came from her being a relative unknown. Suddenly she was thrust into the spotlight and was a fresh face in the political mainstream. No one knew anything about her and people were compelled by her story. Hillary Clinton was a First Lady, then a senator, and was always in the press. But while Clinton was popular, she was also disliked by large sections of the country's middle class who were then drawn to the Alaskan governor. Palin also said what she thought, and was often criticised for doing so. She was controversial, often wrong, and sometimes went off-message. That in itself provided great fodder for reporters because there was always a headline. I saw a few of her rallies and was impressed by her ability to handle the pressure of the big stage without that kind of prior experience. There were rumblings behind the scenes that she was not getting along with John McCain, but you wouldn't have been able to detect any friction between the two because she spoke passionately about her running mate. At least publicly anyway.

Since the unpopular George W. Bush had been side-lined during McCain's campaign, the only Republican party star left to call on was California Governor Arnold Schwarzenegger – or the 'Governator' as he was nicknamed. I caught a rally on a cold night in Columbus, Ohio, where he warmed up the crowd for McCain.

'You all look pumped up,' Arnie said to the roar and laughter of the crowd. He continued with his trademark accent.

As you know, I love Ohio. Every year in March I come here to organise the Arnold Classic, which is the greatest bodybuilding expo in the world. It's all about building up the body and pumping up. That's why, at the next Arnold Classic, I want to invite Senator Obama because he needs to do something about those skinny legs! We're gonna make him do some squats! And then we're going to give him some biceps curls to beef up those scrawny little arms. But if he could only do something about putting some meat on his ideas. Senator McCain, on the other hand, is built like a rock. His character and his views are solid.

Despite his personal failings, Schwarzenegger had charisma in spades, and he gave the McCain campaign a boost. But the attacks kept coming from Obama and McCain couldn't shy away from them. He was seventy-two years old, and the Democrats would remind the crowds that Sarah Palin was just a heartbeat away from being president. In other words, if McCain were elected president and something happened to his health, the completely inexperienced Palin would be the leader of the free world. It was a scare campaign but it worked.

I had read McCain's books and watched his speeches, and I felt that he would have made a good president. He seemed a man of honour, the grandson of one of the US Navy's great commanders during World War II. His father, too, had been a highly respected four-star admiral. McCain number three had picked up where they left off. He spent five and a half years as a prisoner of war in Vietnam after the plane he piloted was shot down over Hanoi in 1968; McCain parachuted right into the Trúc Bạch Lake in the middle of the city.

Unfortunately for John McCain, his run for office came at the wrong time. After the long, bloody and costly years of Iraq and Afghanistan, the United States was war-weary, and the declining economy was causing mounting problems at home. The unpopular end to George W. Bush's presidency also worked against McCain and the Republican chances.

When I saw one of the final Republican rallies in North Carolina, on 1 November 2008 – three days before the election – Sarah Palin tried to steer the rhetoric into positive territory. She pumped her fists on stage as she stood before a crowd of a few hundred people inside a sheltered barn, plus a live televised national audience.

> Our country is facing some tough times right now, tough economic times. Now, more than ever we need someone tough as president. We need a leader with experience, courage, good judgment, and truthfulness. We need someone with a bold, free and fair plan of action, and to take our country in a new direction. We need John McCain now!

But it was clear where this election was heading. It seemed as though it had already been decided long ago. Possibly even way back in 2004 when Obama burst onto the political stage and gave perhaps his most famous keynote speech at the Democratic convention supporting then presidential candidate John Kerry.

> There are those who are preparing to divide us, the spin masters and negative ad peddlers who embrace the politics of anything goes. Well, I say to them tonight, there's not a liberal America and a conservative America; there's the United States of America. There's not a black America and white America and Latino America and Asian America; there's the United States of America. The pundits, the pundits like to slice and dice our country into red states and blue States: red states for Republicans, blue States for Democrats. But I've got news for them, too. We worship an awesome God in the blue states, and we don't like federal agents poking around our libraries in the red states. We coach little league in the blue states and, yes, we've got some gay friends in the red states. There are patriots who opposed the war in Iraq, and there are patriots who supported the war in Iraq. We are one people, all of us pledging allegiance to the stars and stripes, all of us defending the United States of America.

If that was Obama's pitch for the highest office in the land, it was realised four short years later, after a decisive election night on Tuesday, 4 November 2008, when Barack Obama won more votes than any American presidential candidate in history.

•

The crowd swelled with pride. People of different colours and creeds were rugged up in the cold. More than a million people, possibly even two million, stretched along Washington's National Mall from the Capitol Hill building way back to the Washington Monument, and further on towards the Memorial Parks. That's a strip of land totalling a few kilometres that was filled with lively bodies. I'd never seen so many people gathered in the one place at one time. It was 20 January 2009 and it was a vibrant morning for business, too, as vendors set up stalls to sell commemorative badges, magnets, shirts, and little Obama bobble head toys. Of course, being America, there were plenty of hot dog and burger stands as well. People didn't seem to mind the intense security screening and police presence that was in force.

Despite their previous intense rivalry, Obama had nominated Hillary Clinton to be his Secretary of State, his top foreign diplomat, and one of her first tasks in this important role was to deal with the threat posed by terrorists. The incoming Obama and outgoing Bush national security teams met to share concerns about inauguration day, which Hillary Clinton wrote about in her book, *Hard Choices*.

> What if a bomb goes off? Is the Secret Service going to rush him off the podium with the whole world watching? I could see from the look on the faces of the Bush team that nobody had a good answer. For two hours we discussed how to respond to reports of

a credible terrorist threat against the inauguration. The intelligence community believed that Somali extremists associated with al-Shabab, an al-Qaeda affiliate, were trying to sneak across the Canadian border with plans to assassinate the new president. Should we move the ceremony indoors? Cancel it altogether? There was no way we were going to do either. The inauguration had to go forward as planned. The peaceful transfer of power is too important a symbol of American democracy . . . In the end the inauguration went off without incident.

The inauguration was the climax of a celebration that was now into its third day. Festivities began on 18 January with stage performances by Bruce Springsteen, U2, and Beyoncé. They were mixed in with speeches by actors Denzel Washington and Tom Hanks, and the new Vice President Joe Biden. Washington was the place to be.

The National Mall was a scene of history and remembrance and in 2009 another page was being written. It's where Martin Luther King Jr told the world about his dream. It's where protests were held for civil rights and against wars. Popes have led masses there, and rock stars have performed concerts. It's also where presidents were inaugurated, but Obama's inauguration was on a much bigger scale than any before. It was almost beyond belief. It must have been quite a sight for those who were on stage, particularly for Barack Obama, who was about to be sworn in as the forty-fourth

President of the United States. The crowd standing in front of him was the reason he was on stage.

I must have been a kilometre back, and although I could vaguely make out the men and women on stage through my squinted eyes, they resembled tiny dots, so I watched most of the ceremony on large screens that were placed to the side of the audience. There were a few misplaced words in the oath, perhaps a result of nerves, so it had to be retaken at a later date, but no one in the crowd seemed to notice or even care.

The time of the inauguration was ideal for Australia's morning TV viewers and so my brother Karl had been flown in to broadcast it, alongside Rob Penfold, who had covered the vast majority of the Obama campaign. My job was to roam among the crowd and ask questions of the people who were there.

'I think it is probably the most pivotal moment in my lifetime,' said one person.

Another told me through tears, 'Oh I'm feeling historic. This is awesome, what a feeling! This is history and it's just incredible. I've been crying, it's that emotional. America is not just one person, or one race, or one creed. It's for everybody, got it? I love it!'

If Moscow was the coldest place I'd ever been, then Washington DC came in at number two that day. It was bloody freezing. Two and even three layers of clothing weren't enough. We all wore gloves, scarves and overcoats but still needed more. I felt sorry for Karl and Rob who had to present the show and talk for hours with a thick tartan blanket covering their legs.

Americans never really find it difficult to show their emotions in public, and so there they were with their hearts on their sleeves. The crowd chanted 'Obama, Obama, Obama' as the man of the moment walked to the microphone and gave his first inaugural address, which carried the theme of rebuilding America during the height of the economic crisis – the central theme of the long and bitter election campaigns.

The speech lasted for about twenty minutes, and was often interrupted by loud applause and supportive chants. It was received well by the crowd who, despite the historic occasion, shivered in their shoes!

Although it didn't compare with the pomp and pageantry that I'd see at Britain's royal celebrations, such as the marriage of Prince William and Kate Middleton, a presidential inauguration was as close as America came. The country had just elected a new president, and Obama and the new first family – which included his wife Michelle and their young daughters, Sasha and Malia – waved to the crowds as they moved towards the White House. There were colourful marching bands, school processions from Obama's home in Hawaii, dancers, and tumblers. The new first family travelled in the bulletproof presidential vehicle known as 'Cadillac One' before ignoring the advice of the Secret Service to get out on two occasions so they could walk and wave back to the crowds who were walking and running beside them.

While a new president was entering the White House, an old one was heading out as George and Laura Bush prepared to hand over the keys.

It must be a strange feeling to be one of the most powerful men in the world, and then not be. But that is part of what makes a fruitful democracy.

The honeymoon period could only last for so long, though. Work had to be done, and trouble was brewing.

•

When Obama became president, the American economy was in the toilet. It was much worse than a hangover from the Bush years, it turned into national paralysis. Excuses could only last so long. Lives were being ruined. Millions of people had lost their homes and were out of work. People couldn't afford to pay back their loans or their mortgages so they just packed up, left their houses and called it a write-off. The United States wasn't just in recession; it was gripped by an economic disaster that rivalled the Great Depression of 1929. The US dollar had lost so much of its value that it became weaker than the Australian dollar, which hadn't happened in decades. Insurance giants caved in.

All the talk of 'hope' and 'change' had vanished in a few months. I returned to Washington later in 2009 to report from Capitol Hill after the government decided to buy all the bad debt and bail out the big banks. It was highly controversial but apparently the lesser of two evils.

Although it took a while, the bailout worked. But as the US slowly tried to get back on its feet, it was hit by another blow – terror returned to the country.

On 5 November 2009, at a military base in Fort Hood, Texas, a lone gunman named Nidal Hasan opened fire and killed thirteen people including a pregnant soldier; thirty-two others were injured during the ten-minute rampage before Hasan was wounded by two police officers in a shootout. Then aged forty, Hasan shouted '*Allahu Akbar*' as he gunned down his fellow soldiers. Hasan was a medical corps major and a psychologist in the US Army, and was about to be sent to Afghanistan.

The military base was in complete lockdown when I arrived that evening, and the region was understandably still in a state of shock. At the time, the US senate called it the worst terror attack on American soil since 11 September 2001. Like so many of America's mass shooters, Hasan was socially isolated, plus he'd become aggrieved by the war stories he had heard from fellow officers. Hasan was a practising Muslim, and some of his friends later reported that his views had taken on a distinctly anti-American tone. Six months earlier, he had come to the attention of federal authorities after he discussed suicide bombings on internet forums, and viewed radical Islamic websites. The FBI also uncovered an extensive email chain before the attack between Hasan and Anwar al-Awlaki in Yemen. Awlaki had links to the terror group al-Qaeda, and called Hasan a hero in a jihadi blog post afterwards. He said he was 'a man of conscience who could not bear living the contradiction of being a Muslim and serving in an army that is fighting against his own people'.

Hasan's wounds were not fatal, and he recovered in a San Antonio hospital under heavy police guard before he was charged. In 2013, he was convicted of thirteen counts of premeditated murder, thirty-two counts of attempted murder, and was sentenced to death.

Before Hasan's conviction, al-Qaeda had struck again, or at least it tried to, on Christmas Day 2009. A 23-year-old Nigerian named Umar Farouk Abdulmutallab attempted to blow up Northwest Airlines Flight 253 from Amsterdam as it landed in Detroit. Abdulmutallab became known as the 'underwear bomber', as he tried to detonate plastic explosives that were stitched into his underwear. It would have been a disaster on an unimaginable scale, but America – not to mention the 289 people on board – got lucky. The explosive failed to work properly.

Passengers told police Abdulmutallab was in the toilet for about twenty minutes before the plane started its descent. When he came back to his chair he placed a blanket over his legs. Passengers then smelt a foul odour and heard some popping noises before they noticed a small fire on the wall of the plane and from Abdulmutallab's pants. A nearby passenger jumped on him to extinguish the fire. Again, al-Awlaki was linked to the attack, after al-Qaeda claimed responsibility for training the young Nigerian and supplying the explosives.

Abdulmutallab pleaded guilty to charges of attempted use of a weapon of mass destruction, the attempted murder of 289 people, the attempted destruction of a civilian aircraft, and possession of explosives. He was sentenced to four life terms plus fifty years without parole.

•

Obama had delivered on his first promise – 'change' had indeed come to America, in that a new president with new ideas and policies had come to power. But words are one thing; actions are something else. Bush left Obama with a few thumping headaches and his administration struggled to deal with the aftershocks of the 2008 economic meltdown, while thousands of troops were still serving in Iraq and Afghanistan; in this turn fed the hungry bellies of government critics and protesters. Obama eventually restored confidence to the economy but internationally America still had problems, as new conflicts emerged steered by the likes of Bashar al-Assad and Vladimir Putin. But Obama will always point his belligerent critics to the death of terror leader Osama bin Laden, which was a high point of his presidency. He could lay claim to the capture of the world's most wanted man. Something George W. Bush hadn't been able to achieve.

In the United States, gun violence, mass shootings and race riots dominated Obama's years in office, while war and terrorism led his international agenda.

I covered election campaigns in Australia, France, Scotland, Germany, Russia and Ukraine, but none of them came anywhere near the razzle dazzle of the American campaign that produced a leader for the ages. Even though his critics and supporters will debate what he did or didn't achieve, and what his legacy is, they can't deny that he arrived like a force of nature that swept across a ready planet.

In his closing address to the nation on 11 January 1989, Ronald Reagan said: 'Once you begin a great movement, there's no telling where it will end. We meant to change a nation, and instead, we changed a world.'

When he looks back on his years in office, I wonder whether Obama will share a similar opinion. I know I'll at least be glad I had a close-up view.

Chapter 12

DEATH OF THE 'SMOOTH CRIMINAL'

MICHAEL JACKSON ———————————————

The planet stopped spinning on 25 June 2009, the day that Michael Jackson died. At least that's how his fans felt, anyway.

It was one of those 'wow' moments that comes along every so often, when something entirely unexpected catches the world by complete surprise. The biggest 'celebrity death' since Princess Diana. The 'gloved one' was gone and very few people outside his inner circle had seen it coming.

Jackson suffered a cardiac arrest at his rented mansion in the Holmby Hills district of Los Angeles after he was plied with a fatal cocktail of prescription drugs. One of those drugs was the anaesthetic propofol, which is usually only available in hospitals and administered intravenously. Jackson had been preparing to relaunch his career with an ambitious fifty-date concert series in London, but he'd looked a shell of a man in his final weeks and had played a dangerous game with painkillers and sleeping agents. While his body ached in agony after years of torment, his heart ultimately packed it in. He was only fifty.

Although I was based in Los Angeles in 2009, I was in New York at the time of Jackson's death, and even the city that never sleeps screeched to a halt when the news hit.

I was at the famed Madison Square Garden, a stage that Jackson moonwalked across on more than one occasion. But he was not why I was there. I was covering the 2009 NBA draft where young Australian basketballer Patty Mills was about to be selected by one of the big American teams. Patty is a lovely bloke who had a big dream that was about to be realised. I was fortunate enough to be there to tell it.

The draft pick moved into the second round, and then the call about Jackson's death came in. Unfortunately, Patty Mills slid right off the news agenda.

Mark Calvert, the Channel Nine news director at the time, asked me to stay in New York for a night to provide a point of difference to LA. The Jackson story was major world news. Cable TV channels, fan pages, and tabloid websites were struggling to keep up with demand for even a sliver of new information about what had happened. The smallest crumb of a detail was chewed over for hours by talk-show hosts. Music channels filled programs with Jackson's elaborate and classic videos. Call it the Jackson effect. Whatever your opinion of the man, it cannot be denied that he'd made a huge mark on the world and many people were devastated by his untimely passing.

Before Nelson Mandela died a few years later in South Africa, I hadn't seen mourning like it. Grown men and women wailing on the street. Children breaking out into Jackson-esque dance moves in honour of their musical hero. Whether it be Los Angeles, his hometown of Gary in Indiana, or New York City, the images were the same.

Very few events capture the world's attention at the same time so when they do it's a big story. Channel Nine provided rolling coverage of events in LA and people's reactions to Jackson's death throughout most of the day. My responsibilities were to sum up the mood. Speak to the people and relay it all back to our viewers.

I was based outside the famous Apollo Theater in Harlem where a spontaneous wake had formed, attracting thousands of people from across the city. It may not have been LA, where Jackson had lived and spent most of his career, but many New Yorkers claimed to have a spiritual connection to him because New York was where it all began. The first stop on the road to a frighteningly successful career that came with untold riches.

The Apollo Theater calls itself the soul of African American culture. The greats had all played there, from Ella Fitzgerald to Louis Armstrong; gospel supremos such as Sam Cooke as well as soul kings including Ray Charles, Otis Redding and Aretha Franklin. Big, big names. The stage had a certain magic about it. But the jewel in the Apollo's crown may well be that Michael Jackson made his debut there in 1969 as the fresh-faced lead singer of The Jackson 5.

Cameraman Joel Wilson and I were amongst a crowd of deeply depressed Jackson fanatics whose turbo-charged emotions switched regularly from tears of loss and heart-break to celebratory cheers of support and encouragement about the life that was. People of different colour – black or white, as one of his songs was titled – gathered and consoled each other. They didn't care who was watching or listening. Some reached up towards the heavens as an endless stream of Jackson's hits were played on repeat through the venue's speaker system outside. People swayed and sang along. In key or out of key. It didn't matter. It struck me at the time how amazing it was that one person had affected so many.

Above us, a flashing marquee read 'In Memory of Michael Jackson: A true Apollo legend.' Even at four o'clock in the morning local time, when I crossed live into the Nine network's evening news bulletins in Australia, the crowds were still there and still vocal.

In the final years of his life Jackson was plagued by sex abuse lawsuits, relentless paparazzi and rumours of plastic surgery. Despite any personal failings he had or had suffered, I was reminded time and time again that evening at the Apollo Theater, and beyond that night, that Jacko was one of history's greatest pop stars. Recognised around the world. An undisputed musical pioneer, and a philanthropist of epic proportions.

I was back in LA within days but the mourning continued for weeks. Huge queues of fans would gather at his star on the Hollywood Walk of Fame. They stood and sweated in the hot Californian summer sun for hours for a chance to lay a flower, light a candle, or leave a card or a picture with a personal handwritten tribute. Similarly, many people formed queues and took pictures outside the sprawling estate where Jackson died. I imagine that the feeling would have been very much the same when Elvis died in 1977, and then John Lennon three years later.

Just as it was with Presley and Lennon, fans were searching for answers. Why? How?

I reported a few times from the front gates of Jackson's estate, inside a sealed-off section for media, and couldn't help but notice that if he had died close to bankruptcy, as some reports suggested, then by the look of the property he still appeared to be living very well – even if his health was failing and his body shutting down.

Answers to how and why he died would come during the months and years of highly publicised court cases and legal battles, but at the time, it all seemed very tragic.

•

The Jackson story kept me busy for weeks as new details about his life and death trickled to the press. I filed several reports a day for Channel Nine news in the weeks leading up to the final stretch – the star-studded memorial and funeral.

On 7 July 2009, I was towards the back of LA's Staples Center for Jackson's memorial. The centre is where the LA Lakers play basketball and the world's biggest musical acts perform. Jackson had performed in the stadium just two days before his death as he prepared for his *This Is It* tour. The centre holds 20,000 people but I noticed dozens of seats were vacant, a great shame for many a fan who would have loved to have been there.

Michael Jackson's closed, solid bronze casket, plated with fourteen-carat gold, rested in front of the stage. The rest of The Jackson 5 sat close by in the front row. Dressed in black suits, red ties and dark sunglasses – Jermaine, Tito, Jackie and Marlon each wore a single white sequined glove in memory of their youngest brother.

The oddness of the Jackson family is well documented. A family divided by greed and jealousy. But they were thankfully united as the memorial was beamed live to a worldwide television and internet audience running into the hundreds of millions.

Mariah Carey, Stevie Wonder, Usher, and Lionel Ritchie were among the performers singing heartfelt tributes to the man inside the flower-draped coffin just a few metres away.

The memorial had a personal touch. It felt sincere and I was moved. But most people in the room never knew him. So how do you mourn someone you've never met? I suppose his fans felt close to him having followed him for so long. As a kid, I loved MJ's music; who didn't? Now he was gone.

'Michael Jackson went into orbit and never came down,' said Motown Records founder Berry Gordy. He then claimed Jackson was the greatest entertainer who ever lived.

'Maybe now they will leave you alone,' said brother Marlon.

But the family, and the galaxy of big names, were all upstaged by an eleven-year-old girl – Michael Jackson's daughter Paris. I remember feeling sorry for her as she was nudged towards the microphone to offer a few words. Despite pressure, and I'm sure plenty of anxiety, Paris showed courage as she spoke through tears and said, 'I just want to say, ever since I was born, Daddy has been the best father you could ever imagine, and I just want to say I love him so much.' There was a collective sigh in the audience to what became the lingering image of the day. A heartbroken young girl whose father was now a memory.

In Los Angeles, roads and highways are jammed at the best of times, so several streets had to be closed to allow the casket to be driven dozens of kilometres from downtown LA to the beautiful Forest Lawn cemetery in Glendale, close to the Hollywood Hills. News choppers filmed and broadcast the cortege live as Jackson was taken on his final journey. In death, as it was in life, his every move was captured through a lens.

More than seventy days after his funeral, which was also broadcast on TV, Jackson's remains were interred inside a marble crypt at Forest Lawn Memorial Park's Great Mausoleum on 3 September 2009. The land was actually once a Walt Disney filming location and more stars are buried there than at any other place in the world. The park's well-manicured green lawns are dominated with headstones and statues featuring the names from Hollywood's glorious past: Humphrey Bogart, Bette Davis, Nat King Cole and Clark Gable, to name but a few. And now Michael Jackson.

'The king is dead' was the ancient proclamation when the monarch of the French royal family passed away. 'Long live the king' was then declared in support of his successor. As the King of Pop, Jackson sat untouched on the golden musical throne for most of his life. But his stature was so significant, up there with The Beatles and Elvis Presley, that there was no successor. The King of Pop was dead and it's still argued that a new musical monarch is yet to be crowned.

•

Jackson's spirit had sailed and his body was long gone but the whole sorry saga was far from over. A strange sideshow was about to begin that would shed new light on the pop star's life and death. It seemed a sideshow always accompanied Michael Jackson.

Attention turned to Jackson's personal physician, Dr Conrad Murray, who was the last person to see him alive. Murray was with the entertainer on the night he died and administered the potent and deadly cocktail of sedatives that caused Jackson's heart attack.

The police dragnet was closing in and the doctor's Las Vegas offices were raided some months after the funeral.

But it wasn't until the following year that an arrest and charge came.

I dipped in and out as I covered the Murray story over the next few months, which included some trips to Las Vegas when his medical practice was raided by police, as well as his surrender at Los Angeles Superior Court on a charge of involuntary manslaughter on 8 February 2010. Prosecutors filed a criminal complaint that alleged Murray acted 'unlawfully, and without malice to kill Michael Joseph Jackson' by administering the surgical anaesthetic propofol and other tranquillisers to the singer. The coroner's report had already revealed Jackson died of 'acute propofol intoxication' as the dosage of propofol was sufficient for major surgery.

It has to be said, Michael Jackson's fans are a crazy bunch. They are known for it. They blindly followed whatever he said and whatever he did. If music is religion, then he was their god. So, just as they stood by him in life, they would do the same in death, and sure, I was impressed with the loyalty and tenacity of his fans. Like those at the Apollo Theater in New York months before, their grief was still palpable and their determination to find answers was unwavering. Without fail, Jackson's fans were out the front of the court, loyal to the end with signs demanding answers.

Murray was from Trinidad and Tobago and became pals with Jackson in 2006 after the doctor helped take care of Jackson's children in Las Vegas. Three years later, as Jackson readied himself for the gruelling fifty-date London concert series, he employed Murray on a staggering wicket of about US$150,000 a month. Apparently Murray was the only person the pop star trusted outside his three children. Perhaps it was because he couldn't say no to Jackson's heavy reliance on drugs. Jackson, it appears, had become an insomniac, and others wouldn't give him what he craved because they feared he might not wake up. Murray didn't seem to share their fear.

On 25 June 2009, at 10.50 am, Murray gave Jackson the fatal dose. Then the doctor went to the bathroom. Two minutes later he returned and Jackson had stopped breathing. Murray conducted CPR on the bed. Even I would know to conduct CPR on a hard surface rather than a bouncy mattress, but that's what the doctor did. Murray freaked out. He made a number of phone calls to different people, including Jackson's personal assistants and personal security, before eventually dialling 911. In fact, about ninety minutes passed before an ambulance was called. By that time Jackson had no chance. He was rushed to UCLA Medical Center but by 2.30 in the afternoon he was dead.

A police search of Jackson's property revealed just how deep into addiction Jackson was. They found bottles of anti-depressants, anti-anxiety medications, anti-pain and insomnia drugs, which included Valium, Flomax, Ativan and Restoril, all prescribed by Murray. Turns out Jackson couldn't live with or without drugs. It was a lose–lose situation.

The case continued far beyond my time in the United States. In the middle of 2010 I was transferred to the London bureau to act as the network's Europe, Middle East and Africa correspondent. I watched from afar as the windows to Jackson's sad strange life were thrust wide open. Ultimately, Murray was convicted of the crime and sentenced to four years in prison.

Jackson's life was certainly unique. Very few stars reach the dizzy heights that he did in a career that spanned several decades. From a poor child star in the Indiana suburbs to the world conquering highest-selling artist of all time. But in later years he became a punchline. By the time he announced the comeback tour he was desperate for cash. Along with his ridiculously extravagant lifestyle, enablers fleeced off his vast fortune. But it was the child abuse allegations that hurt the most. The scandals were many and damaging, and then there were the drugs. It seems as though this was another case of someone who seemed to have it all, but he died relatively young and lonely. If there's an upside, it's that his music survived, and that, to his fans, is what soars louder and longer than anything else.

Chapter 13

BEAUTY SPRINGS FROM AN UGLY END

THE FUNERALS OF NEPAL

Men, women, and children formed long queues. Each of them was wrapped in a white sheet. But the sheet wasn't protecting them from the cold, or the sun, it was preserving whatever dignity they had left. Because the long queues of people wrapped in sheets were dead. Killed in a sudden and extreme circumstance. Their souls had left their bodies and drifted into the great unknown. The wrapped bundles were awaiting cremation on funeral pyres. Thousands had already been burned; thousands more were still to come.

It was 29 April 2015 and I was on the banks of Nepal's Bagmati River, which was a murky brown stream that split the Kathmandu Valley. Old temples and a rich green forest surrounded it, and wild monkeys roamed with curious abandon. Hindus and Buddhists thought the river was a holy place; they believed it purified the people spiritually and had done for thousands of years. The city certainly needed something healing at such a terrible time.

A deadly earthquake, measuring 7.8 on the Richter scale, had just hit Nepal – a tourist mecca and one of the poorest nations on earth. Since the epicentre was at a relatively shallow depth of fifteen kilometres below ground, the earthquake's impact was maximised and the carnage was devastating. It was similar to what had happened in Haiti in 2010. Nepal lies on a fault line, so tremors are not uncommon, but the quake on 25 April 2015 struck with such force and intensity that it became the country's worst natural disaster in more than eighty years.

The earthquake struck four minutes before midday, the busiest part of the day, when locals and tourists were milling about and preparing lunch. In Kathmandu, and many towns beyond, buildings swayed and monuments crashed to the ground, roofs caved in and walls tumbled down. People darted past each other and around the falling masonry – a desperate dash for life. Some lost their balance on the splitting roads. It must have seemed apocalyptic. The only thing that wasn't moving was the sky. All it took was fifty seconds from the first sway to the last rattle to crush the Nepalese capital.

The earthquake's epicentre was in the district of Lamjung, near the centre of Nepal, and the chaos and destruction stretched far and wide, from the built-up city of Kathmandu to the isolated farmlands, way out to Mount Everest. Sherpas call Everest 'Mother of the World', but she wouldn't spare some of the climbers trapped on her icy ridges and snowy valleys. The unexpected tremor triggered a landslide – a white wave of thick powder surged down the mountain like a pack of charging bulls and enveloped groups of climbers. At least nineteen people were killed. It was one of the earthquake's violent tentacles, and many people were stuck on Everest for days.

It would be several more hours before I, and much of the world, knew this was happening. I was in Channel Nine's Sydney newsroom, and it was just after 6 pm when news about the quake started breaking. Because earthquakes happen all the time, a mission isn't given the go-ahead until we know the extent of the damage. Although a quake in Nepal already had our attention because of the likelihood that Australians would be caught up in it. Nepal is a major attraction for Australian climbers.

It was the next morning, Australian time, when the call came from Sydney news director Simon Hobbs that I would be on the next plane to Nepal. The aircraft would be Malaysian Airlines, which wasn't great for my flight anxiety. As we crossed Western Australia and over the Indian Ocean where flight MH370 went missing, I spent hours chewing my nails and closely watching the flight path on the TV to see if the plane veered off course! We stopped in Kuala Lumpur and then connected through to Kathmandu, but because there was so much emergency air traffic in Nepal we were caught in a holding pattern and circled the capital for two hours before we could land. It was go time, as soon as we touched down.

I met dozens of Australians who were trapped in the chaos. They had all feared for their lives and painted frightening pictures for me as they described the harrowing sounds of a rolling quake.

Susan Welch told me, 'You've just got no control over it. You've just got to get out to open spaces as fast as you can.'

Peter Nicholson said, 'For the first few seconds I thought I was going crazy, like I was about to faint because I couldn't walk properly. Then I heard all the sound come through, and looked at the buildings and the power lines. People were falling off their motorbikes because they couldn't control them.'

Marie Nicholson was at the Australian consulate when I met her. She was with dozens of others Australians who had nowhere else to go and were awaiting emergency flights home. 'I could feel this rumble underneath my feet. It was slight to start with and then it got louder. It was like a subway underneath me as I heard this loud roar.'

Sandy Ward was in the same situation and told me, 'I have to say I was terrified and literally got pushed out of the shop I was in. The road was going up and down and I thought I was going to die.'

In the midst of the chaos and confusion, rescue workers fanned out across the city. Rescue teams had raced to Nepal from all over the world, from Britain, France, India, the United States, and Australia. Some of them had trained search dogs to get in to places humans couldn't. The dead were pulled from the rubble, their lifeless bodies and expressionless faces covered in grey soot. But where there was grief and despair, occasionally there were also slivers of joy as survivors were heard buried underneath pieces of broken timber. Occasionally members of search teams would drop to their knees and place their ears on the ground. They would shout for people to be quiet so they could listen for something, any sign of life. A shout. A scream. A desperate tap or a kick against the rubble.

Kathmandu was warm during the day and cold at night, as opposed to Haiti, which was tropical around the clock. I suppose the heat may have been of some benefit to the rescue workers who'd come from all over the world. The warmer climate meant rescue teams weren't slowed down by big and bulky clothing, but the heat meant dead bodies decayed at a faster rate, and so the smell became pungent quickly. In Nepal, as in Haiti, I watched humankind at its heart-stopping best as people from different races who spoke different languages worked together to remove debris piece by piece and get survivors out. The survival stories were breathtaking. A mother or a child found alive after twenty-four, forty-eight, sometimes ninety-six hours or more. Each rescue briefly lifted the hearts of the increasingly dispirited rescuers. But the stories became rarities as time went on.

The carnage was worst in the historic city of Bhaktapur, which is about twenty kilometres outside Kathmandu, and about fifty kilometres from the earthquake epicentre.

I walked around, surveying the damage, to file a report for the news that night. Old temples that had stood for hundreds of years were now in pieces. The facades of royal palaces were ruined while statues of Hindu gods had tumbled. Tall monuments with elaborate carvings, pagodas, and religious shrines all formed a scrap heap. The rain was coming down too, which made walking dangerous because there were so many power lines drooping low. Apartments had fallen into each other – not just a few homes, whole streets had been razed. Sides of buildings had been torn away while red brick walls and wooden balconies had crumbled. From the narrow lanes outside, I could see into what were once family homes – kitchens, living rooms and bedrooms with pictures that hung on whatever flimsy wall was left. The whole city looked like a demolition site.

The human cost in Bhaktapur wasn't as significant as Kathmandu, but one-third of the town's infrastructure was wiped out. So many people lived in close quarters and most of the bodies were buried deep in the rubble. In the end, 333 people lost their lives in the district, which was a fraction of the overall death toll.

I watched as rescue workers delicately trod over the piles of debris in the hope of finding trapped survivors. It was a dangerous task because the piles were a soup of material – large pieces of concrete brick and timber – and if the wrong part was stepped on, a rescuer could fall through and sustain bad injuries.

Josh Martin, one of my two cameramen for the trip, had brought a portable remote-controlled drone with him, which allowed us to film and survey the damage from high above. If the devastation looked bad on the ground, it was worse from a bird's-eye view. The drone gave a brutally stunning perspective of the damage from the ancient city of Bhaktapur way out to the Nepalese mountain ranges. A country of such serene beauty had become a new hell. The drone is such an effective tool for modern-day storytelling in the days immediately following a natural disaster that I don't think I'd cover another such event without one. In days gone by, film crews would rely on expensive helicopter rides to film damage from the sky. The drone, if its use is permitted by local authorities, is a much cheaper and easier alternative.

As with Haiti in 2010, the ugly side of nature had struck the poorest. An estimated twenty-eight million people lived below the poverty line in Nepal. That's the population of Australia, and then some, getting by on just a few dollars a day. Nepalese are a proud people, but life was about to get much harder.

In those fifty seconds, 8583 people were killed; that's 160 every second. More than 600,000 homes were destroyed, so most of the victims were killed inside as roofs caved in, pinning bodies to the ground. Which brings us to the muddy banks of the Bagmati River.

I'd seen large clouds of black smoke rising into the air over the ancient Hindu temples, and wondered what it was.

I assumed it must have been a crushed building that had caught fire. My driver told me that the smoke was from funerals. The bodies of the dead were being burned in mass cremations. It's Hindu custom to bury the dead as soon as possible because Hindus believe it helps the soul escape quickly from the body. But because there were so many bodies to cremate, it became a desperate attempt to observe and maintain tradition while avoiding the spread of disease.

I asked the driver if we could take a look. As we got closer, the smoke plumes became taller, and the smell began to waft. That sickly unmistakable smell of rotting corpses. I was with cameramen Josh Martin and Ollie Clarke, and we all put masks on our faces.

I didn't plan on watching the funerals, as grieving families said goodbye to their lost loved ones, but, with the greatest respect, I couldn't turn away. I'd never seen anything like it before and I was touched.

I stood from a short distance and observed. Lines of bodies wrapped in white cotton sheets lay on bare concrete beside the river. One by one, they were picked up and carried to the edge of the Bagmati River where pyres had been placed on about half-a-dozen concrete pillars. Nepalese families who had money could pay for the use of the concrete pillars, whereas those who were poor could only burn the bodies in the river's muddy flats.

I watched the funeral of a middle-aged man. I didn't know his story, or how he died, or whom he left behind. The fact that he was there said enough.

Priests, or funeral leaders, unwrapped the body and then cut off the man's clothing, which left him naked except for his underwear. Most of the time, the unwrapping revealed horrific injuries from whatever object had landed on top of the person. But the middle-aged man had no visible wounds. Perhaps he had been struck across the head. At least it would have been quick.

The body was then wiped with cloth and cleaned with water to prepare it for the next stage. Because there was such a large queue of bodies, and the male funeral leaders were busy, this was done rather quickly and not with great precision – but the intent was there. Next the body was rewrapped in white cloth – a colour that often means purification. Then came a second wrapping. In the man's case, it was an orange sari or traditional cloth over the white cotton sheet. After this, a chain of marigolds was placed on the orange sari. Marigolds are beautiful orange flowers that play a big part in Nepalese culture as they are often kept in houses and used for rituals.

The body was then placed on salwood logs, stacked in a rectangular shape about half a metre high. This was the base. Next, the body burner sprinkled red powder over the body, and tossed in some packets of ghee (clarified butter), which helped speed the cremation. The last goodbye from family members came next; a goodbye these families could never have expected just a few days ago.

I looked to my left and saw similar funerals taking place, and when I looked to my right, I saw even more. There were hundreds of people – families who had just said goodbye and others who were preparing to. Grey skies at sunset matched the downcast mood. Not much was said as people, most of whom wore masks over their mouths, quietly acknowledged each other's shared grief. They shuffled along the riverbank while up above, on the temple roofs, monkeys chased after each other oblivious to the deep mourning at ground level. The little rascals had seen plenty over the years.

My eyes returned to the funeral I had been watching. Once the body was placed on the dried wood, the families gathered around and circled it. One by one, they bowed their head, said a prayer, and moved on in a clockwise direction. I watched a lady, who I assumed to be a mother, speak to her lost son as tears streamed down her face. A family friend placed a supportive hand around her back. Some members did one lap of the body, while others did a few. Some people even placed a few coins and some paper money on the chest of the body. Once the family and friends of the deceased had said what they wanted to say, they left the concrete pillar and stood nearby on the concrete footpath to watch the completion of the ceremony, or what people in Nepal believe to be the person's final journey into the eternal world. The soul was being guided to its next destination.

As mourners quietly sobbed into their handkerchiefs, the body burner placed sticks of incense around the body to help sweeten the smell. Large handfuls of dried straw were then carefully placed on top of the orange-clad body to cover it up, and to help the fire take hold. The straw was an important part of the process to make sure the cremation happened smoothly and relatively quickly. To keep the straw in position, a few more short pieces of heavy timber were placed on top. If a priest was there a final prayer was said, and then the body burner lit a stick and placed it on the straw.

It didn't seem to take long for the fire to take hold and for smoke to spiral into the acrid air. Strangely enough, the smell wasn't what I thought it would be. There was no distinct odour from burning flesh; it was mostly just smoke from the burning wood, which stuck to our clothes and followed us. It must have taken just a few minutes before the pyre was well alight. The family stood side by side and watched as the body was burned and the man's soul moved on to whatever world awaited him.

About twenty minutes after the pyre was lit, the sari, the marigold, and the body had all been consumed by the flames and all that was left behind were ashes. The scattered remains of a dark grey ash rested on the blackened concrete pillar. But it wasn't over just yet. The crowds began to disperse but the last part of the ritual was still to come. The funeral leader or body burner swept the ashes together and then pushed it all into the Bagmati River. That's what made the waterway so sacred. Millions of Nepalese had been dissolved into the river's waters for centuries. That final act was the last great honour. The soul had left the body, and the capsule for the soul had returned to the river and joined his forebears.

I'd been to many funerals around the world. In the Middle East I saw dozens of them. Similar to the religious protocol and custom in Nepal, the bodies had to be buried quickly. In Gaza and Libya, crowds of Muslims would carry the bodies of the dead, running up the streets to wherever the cemetery was. Again, the body would be wrapped in a white sheet before it was lowered into a grave and buried.

But in Nepal there was something gentle and peaceful about it all. I'm certain the families didn't want to be burying their loved ones, especially under such horrific circumstances, but while it was tragic and awful, there seemed to be an acceptance of death and I found the goodbyes truly beautiful.

•

For a devastated family, burying a loved one did not necessarily mean the end of their tragedy. That's the sad truth of living on a fault line. The hits keep on coming. When there is one major earthquake, there are usually several more aftershocks. As I knew from Haiti, aftershocks could be even more violent than the original earthquake. The slightest shake or the softest pop could send people running for their lives. Usually, more people were added to the death toll.

Just as I had seen in Haiti, families packed up their belongings and moved to open fields. Thousands of people set up tents and camped by the sides of roads, or looked for parks and farmlands, anywhere without a roof or something hard that might fall and crush them. We spoke to many of the families and, despite not knowing when they might return home, they always greeted us with a smile. I played football with the kids who didn't seemed terribly fazed about where they were. The children also loved watching Josh fly his drone. As it soared into the air and buzzed away, the kids chased after it, laughing loudly in its trail. It made for some terrific heart-warming pictures that we featured in one of our reports.

A few days after the earthquake, I was in Kathmandu talking to an Australian filmmaker who had captured on video the earthquake tremors, and buildings being pushed to the ground. We were having a beer together, and then the earth shook. It took a few moments before we realised exactly what was going on. Someone screamed and ran for the open, while others were stumbling over chairs and crashing into tables to get out. I got moving pretty fast. It might have looked slightly comical as we lunged for safety, but when an aftershock hit, people would do whatever they could to get out from underneath buildings. A survival instinct kicked in and it was every man for himself. Fortunately, we weren't too far away from an unsheltered grassy patch and made it there in relatively quick time. We were joined by dozens of others. We looked at each other, and once it was clear that everyone was okay, we laughed nervously, uttered a few colourful expletives, and hung outside for a little longer. Longer than a little while.

•

The child was alive, but only just. His little chest gently rose and fell as his lungs filled with air that was supplied manually by a breathing device that was squeezed by the boy's forlorn mother. His wounds were so severe that he couldn't breathe on his own. The plastic contraption was all that kept his heart beating. The boy was on a gurney, lying on his side with his eyes closed. A bandage was wrapped around his chest while the air tube was inserted through his mouth. He was in the emergency ward of the main hospital and was in the so-called 'code red' room – the triage area reserved for the most critical patients.

Let me tell you, the code red room of a hospital after an earthquake is as desperate a place as you will find anywhere. It was so harrowing, I couldn't stay for long.

An Australian nurse had brought us to the hospital. A thirty-year-old woman named Lucy Rowe from Newtown in Sydney who worked for a company called Nurse Teach Reach, which trained and educated foreign nurses in foreign lands such as Nepal where good training was needed. Good training was certainly needed in April 2015, when inexperienced local nurses were thrust into a major emergency and could go days without sleep. 'They've found it really stressful. They are tired, and they are exhausted,' Lucy said.

She introduced me to several of the doctors, most of whom were foreigners working incredibly hard under extreme conditions. For many of the patients, those doctors were the bridge between life and death. In the *Oxford Dictionary*, a hero is defined as 'a person who is admired for their courage, outstanding achievements, or noble qualities'. I saw many heroes that day.

Lucy showed me around the different wards, including those inside the hospital and the makeshift triage areas outside where tarpaulins were used for shelter from the hot sun. Lucy attended to the many victims who had varying degrees of injuries. That boy who needed the breathing bag in the code red room was one of the most critical patients of the day, but he wasn't the only one in need of help. I saw a tiny girl who looked to be about five years old, sitting in a daze with a bloody bandage wrapped around her head. There were elderly patients with facial injuries and crushed ankles. There was a seven-year-old boy named Anish Tamain who had two broken legs, the X-ray images showed the clean snap of his femurs.

More wounded from outlying areas where there were no medical facilities were being driven to the hospital in utes. Medical procedures were being carried out on the floor, often without anaesthetic. Could you imagine that? The pain the victims were already in, some of them for days, to then undergo surgery on the ground without painkillers because resources were so stretched. But the doctors didn't have a choice. The little morphine that was available was given to the patients who were in the most pain.

We saw the friends and parents of many victims quietly sobbing in the hospital corridors. The mother who had to manually squeeze air into her son's mouth must have expected the worst, but clung to the smallest of hopes that a god was looking down on her and that maybe her son would pull through. But God didn't seem to be terribly interested in the hospital. Lucy told me it was almost certain that the boy would not make it. His chest was crushed and his body wasn't strong enough to get himself through. 'Families are ventilating their loved ones,' she told me. 'The emotional side of that gets me every time . . . to be breathing for your mum, dad or daughter.'

It was such a heartbreaking scenario, but I was humbled to see the extraordinary work being performed by people who expected nothing in return. I'd seen it time and time again in conflicts and natural disasters around the world. The people who work for many government or non-government organisations, such as Médecins Sans Frontières, are typically selfless and driven people who put themselves in harm's way to at least try to get a country and its people back on their feet. Lucy Rowe summed up that determination and commitment with this parting quote: 'I can't walk away and say that's enough for today. I have to keep going.'

In my experience, that's very much the mindset of the Nepalese people; keep going and keep smiling. No matter the hardships, whether it's climbing a mountain or recovering from earthquakes, keep going. It's the kind of positivity that makes not just the place magical but the people, too, and magic endures. Every brick in Nepal is part of its history. It's all part of Nepal's unique charm. When a brick comes down, it doesn't stay down. It will go back up again.

EPILOGUE

The news trickled in, slowly at first, and it was bad. Really bad. BOMBING IN PARIS. AT LEAST TEN DEAD. I knew it would get worse. It always does. Islamic extremists had opened fire at a rock concert and dozens more were killed. Then came news of other awful co-ordinated attacks. This was a big one. I scrolled through Twitter for any new crumb of detail. Usually I would scurry to my room, pack my bag, call for a cab and head to the airport – but not this time.

It was November 2015, I was in Sydney, and the biggest story since I left bureau life was underway. It was a strange feeling knowing that I wouldn't be covering it. That rush. That adrenaline charge. The addiction that comes with covering a major breaking story washed over me. I felt the pull like a former smoker resisting the urge for one more cigarette.

I snapped out of it. I had to. Because I was on the air in my new job, and while I was thousands of kilometres away from the blasts at the Bataclan I still had an important role to play – one that was every bit as important. I was anchoring the news on the *Weekend Today* show and was part of a team now covering the biggest story in the world. This was my first time on the other side of the camera, asking questions to the journalists and experts from the studio chair. I was buzzing. I remember watching the late great Peter Jennings broadcast so calmly during 9/11, and so I hoped one day to be able to do the same. Not to get caught up in the emotion of the story but to present in a calm, thoughtful, and truthful manner. There were, after all, many victims, and information for our viewers had to be correct. As the death toll passed 130, ad breaks were cancelled and the show was lengthened by several hours. Coffee supplies soared. The order from the control room was to talk. Inform. I was with fellow hosts Cameron Williams, Deborah Knight, and Natalia Cooper, and we crossed from one to another as new details emerged. This is where my experience came into play. I knew Paris. I knew terrorism. I knew ISIS. I'd been there before and covered similar stories, so was able to share that knowledge with the audience. I may not have been on the ground – which is where I'd always prefer to be – but this was the next best thing.

I remember saying to my London producer, Eliza Berkery, after we covered the *Charlie Hebdo* attacks, that there would likely be a lot of other similar events. Random attacks by small groups of extremists that were hard to police.

A few months after Paris came Brussels. Again, I was on the *Today* show. Again I was able to offer some insight. It's something I hope to continue. While I'm not on the ground, I read and read. International news is still my favourite flavour.

I had been overseas during a memorable period of history, reporting on instability and turbulence. It was challenging – and it was exciting. It was a time when the world changed, and so it changed me – not just professionally, but it humbled me as a person and educated me more than I could have imagined. One of my proudest achievements, on top of the stories, was reopening the London bureau after it had been closed for several years. The bureau had been just James and me to begin with. It was new and it was tough but we made it work. Now there are two reporters, two camera operators, and a producer in London.

To be a correspondent was a great honour and something I never took for granted. I spent almost eight years with my foot on the accelerator and hardly took a breather. Which is why I needed to stop, at least for a while. As great as it all is, it's also very taxing on the body and the brain – the constant news coverage, the time-zone changes, and the isolation. The toughest decision I ever made was to let it go. As great as the work is, there comes a time when you feel the pull of home and family. I also felt the urge to try something else and take on a new challenge.

The important thing for me is not just to stay in the business, but to keep moving forward. The challenge now is to learn new broadcasting techniques and expand my set of skills in the journalism industry. It's already helped when I've hosted the *Today* show which has been a great thrill and honour to work for a show that is such a staple of Australian TV history. It allows me to stay close to breaking news and the adrenaline-charged live television format. There is a wonderful excitement that comes with hosting the *Today* show, especially when a major international or domestic news story is unfolding. Switching gears and then moving from a hard interview to something softer is also up my alley because as a correspondent I covered a great range of stories so needed to be quite versatile.

The foreign experience has also helped when I've reported for *60 Minutes*, which has been another great honour. I grew up watching George Negus, Ray Martin, Jeff McMullen and Richard Carleton travel the world and tell great stories, so it's always a privilege when a call comes in. Former *60 Minutes* executive producer Tom Malone gave me a few stories while I was away, and new EP Kirsty Thomson has given me more. What I like about the program is time – hence the clock. More time to get to know the talent, more time on a story, and more time for an interview. The longer interview is a dance I also enjoy.

There is so much more to tell. Terror attacks and a bloody siege in Toulouse; Silvio Berlusconi and his 'bunga bunga' parties; California wildfires of 2009; anniversaries in Berlin and Auschwitz; three Olympics – Vancouver, London, and Sochi; the engagement of Prince William and

Kate Middleton and their famous royal wedding; the night I met the Queen and Prince Philip at Buckingham Palace; Australian racehorse Black Caviar beating the world at Royal Ascot; Ashes tests, World Cups, Academy Awards and Golden Globes. And I hope there is much more still to come. But they are stories for another day.

ACKNOWLEDGEMENTS

No one takes a journey by themselves and there are many great and wonderful people I met along the way. I'd like to thank a few different families, starting with my own. Mum and Dad, TC and Marcus, Karl and Cass, Tom and Jenziiiieeeee – your love and support is always appreciated and reciprocated. Sylvia came along late in the piece but I'm sure glad you did *mi amor* (wink emoji). Thank you for your love, encouragement, and your computer! My main moon Monte, thank you pal. To my manager, Sharon Finnigan, and the team at Hachette Australia including Robert Watkins and Karen Ward – this truly couldn't have been done without you all.

The next family is my Channel Nine family, starting with my bureau cameramen James Gillings, Rich Moran, Luke Wilson, Glenn Edwards, and Joel Wilson. Thanks for the high quality, the hard work, and the laughs, lads!

I'll be forever grateful to Darren Wick, whose sleep I often interrupted, and who rarely said no to a trip or story. Thanks to David Gyngell and John Westacott, who took a punt on me at 26 and sent me to LA, and then Mark Calvert who thought I was the right man to reopen London – thanks,

Guv'nor! I once asked Rob Penfold how he begins a story. He told me he always starts it the same way he'd tell a stranger on the street. Just some of his words I haven't forgotten. I often sought Rob's advice – particularly when reopening the London bureau – and it was always correct. So thank you, Robbie, it's great to be your friend. Thanks also to the LA team including Noel, Carla, Tania, and Lizzie.

Big ups also for my foreign fixers, including Giulia Sirignani, Ameera Harouda, and my security consultants including Shaun, Tony and Russ – thanks for keeping me alive!

Thanks to my foreign editors over the years, starting with David McCombe, who was hard on me at first, but needed to be. Thanks, 'Mullet', for teaching me the power of good writing. Also thanks to Mary Davison, Wes Hardman, Ed Habershon, Michaela Marshall, and Matty Bachl, Michelle Pike, Geoff Pyke and Georgina Jannings in the Nine News library for helping me revisit old stories. A special thank you to my London warrior and producer Eliza Berkery, who I think slept less than I did!

Thanks also to Tom Malone, Stephen Taylor, Kirsty Thomson, and Fiona Dear, who've all given me chances and help along the way. Finally, to Gus and Casey, Nick Atkins, Holly Alina and Michael Valvo, Shawry and Panch, Emma and Henry Zalapa – thanks for looking out for me and giving me a life away from work.

My shout at the bar next!

Peter Stefanovic was the Europe, United States, Africa and Middle East correspondent for the Nine Network. He reported from the scene of major news events around the world for *Nine News*, the *Today* show, and *A Current Affair*. In 2014 Peter was nominated for a Walkley Award for his coverage of the war in Gaza. He is currently a journalist at the Nine Network and a contributor to *60 Minutes*.

 peterstefanovic

 peter_stefanovic